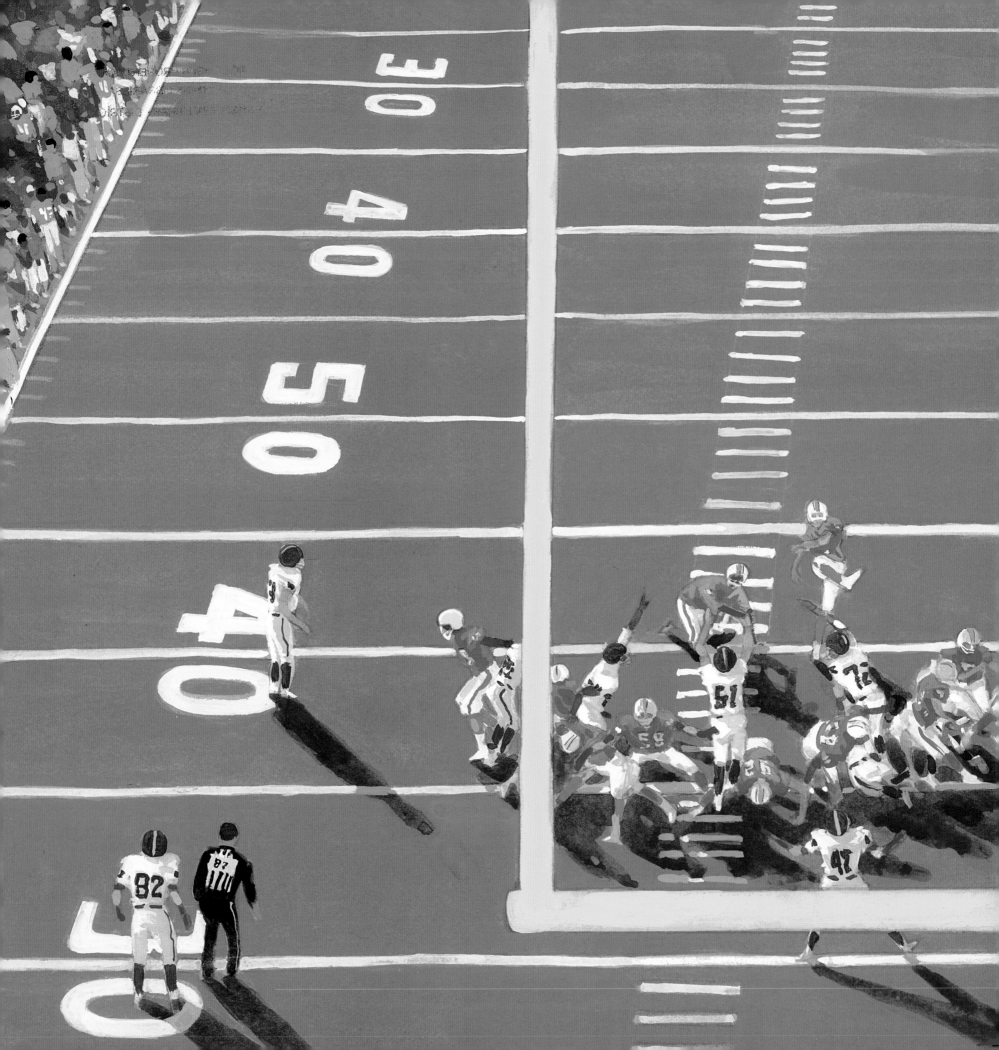

GRIDIRON

GRIDIRON

STORIES FROM 100 YEARS
OF THE NATIONAL FOOTBALL LEAGUE

WRITTEN BY
FRED BOWEN

ILLUSTRATED BY
JAMES E. RANSOME

MARGARET K. McELDERRY BOOKS • NEW YORK LONDON TORONTO SYDNEY NEW DELHI

MARGARET K. McELDERRY BOOKS • An imprint of Simon & Schuster Children's Publishing Division •
1230 Avenue of the Americas, New York, New York 10020 • Text copyright © 2020 by Fred Bowen •
Illustrations copyright © 2020 by James Ransome • All rights reserved, including the right of reproduction
in whole or in part in any form. • MARGARET K. McELDERRY BOOKS is a trademark of Simon & Schuster,
Inc. • For information about special discounts for bulk purchases, please contact Simon & Schuster Special
Sales at 1-866-506-1949 or business@simonandschuster.com. • The Simon & Schuster Speakers Bureau
can bring authors to your live event. For more information or to book an event, contact the Simon & Schuster
Speakers Bureau at 1-866-248-3049 or visit our website at www.simonspeakers.com. • The text for this
book was set in Bulmer MT. • The illustrations for this book were rendered in watercolor. • Manufactured
in China • 0520 SCP • First Edition • 10 9 8 7 6 5 4 3 2 1 • Library of Congress Cataloging-
in-Publication Data • Names: Bowen, Fred, author. | Ransome, James, illustrator. • Title: Gridiron :
stories from 100 years of the National Football League / written by Fred Bowen ; illustrated by James E.
Ransome. • Description: New York : Margaret K. McElderry Books, 2020. | Includes bibliographical
references and index. | Audience: Ages 8–12 | Audience: Grades 4–6 | Summary: "Stories from 100
years of the NFL, from its scrappy beginnings to its greatest players, coaches, and games."—Provided
by publisher. • Identifiers: LCCN 2019038490 (print) | ISBN 9781481481120 (hardcover) | ISBN
9781481481144 (eBook) • Subjects: LCSH: National Football League—History—Juvenile literature. |
Football—United States—History—Juvenile literature. • Classification: LCC GV955.5.N35 B694 2020
(print) | DDC 796.332/640973—dc23 • LC record available at https://lccn.loc.gov/2019038490

PREGAME
SHOW

*J*ared Goff steps to the line of scrimmage. He looks left and right. It's second down and ten yards to go. The Los Angeles Rams are on the New England Patriots twenty-seven yard line, trailing 10–3 with just over four minutes remaining.

The New England defense has dominated the Rams high-powered offense for the entire game. But Los Angeles still has a chance if they can make just one big play.

A television producer sits in a nearby truck and calmly gives orders to the camera operators bringing the game to almost 100 million football fans around the country.

"Let's go to camera three, then to camera four. Ten stay ready."

The 70,081 fans inside the futuristic Mercedes-Benz Stadium in Atlanta, Georgia, as well as thousands of reporters lean forward. Patriots quarterback Tom Brady cranes his neck from the New England sidelines to see the action. Adam Levine of Maroon 5, who performed at halftime and is now in one of the stadium luxury boxes, stops talking and looks toward the field.

"Hut one, hut two. . . ."

Goff gets the ball and steps back. His receivers scatter downfield. The Patriots are blitzing, crashing past the Rams offensive line to get to the quarterback.

1

Goff looks right and spies wide receiver Brandin Cooks racing upfield to the Patriots end zone. He lets the ball fly just as a New England defender flashes by.

The ball hangs in the air a split second too long. Patriots defensive back Stephon Gilmore leaps high in front of Cooks. He grabs the ball and tumbles to the ground.

Interception! Patriots ball at their own four yard line.

The crowd at Mercedes-Benz Stadium explodes in cheers as millions of others dance and scream in front of TVs all over the world. They sense Tom Brady and the Patriots will win again. A record sixth championship.

It's the Super Bowl. The most popular sporting event in America.

It's professional football. The National Football League. The NFL. The most popular sports league in the United States.

Pro football wasn't always like this, with the sellout crowds, television coverage, and high-flying action. But that's another story. In fact, that's a whole lot of stories.

The stories of the NFL. The stories of the . . . Gridiron.

FIRST
QUARTER

1

A NEW LEAGUE

Ralph Hay was a man on the go. At the beginning of the 1920s he owned the biggest automobile dealership in Canton, Ohio, selling Jordans, Hupmobiles, and Pierce-Arrows. Hay dressed in the best suits money could buy and was always smoking a fine cigar.

Hay also owned the Canton Bulldogs professional football team. The rough-and-tumble game was becoming more popular around Ohio, and Hay was one of the first to be in on the action. In 1919 the Bulldogs, led by Jim Thorpe, were the best football team around, winning all their games but one, a tie with the Hammond All-Stars.

Thorpe was a player. He could run the ball, kick the ball, and tackle like a demon. Thorpe was such a terrific all-around athlete that at the 1912 Summer Olympics, he'd won the gold medal in the pentathlon and decathlon.

Even though Hay had the best team and the best player, he still lost money on the Bulldogs.

The game of pro football was a mess. Players played for several teams, jumping from team to team, playing under different names, trying to make some extra money. Teams snuck college players onto their rosters. Some would even grab high school kids from the sidelines to play.

For years there had been talk of creating a real professional football league. Hay decided to make it happen.

He called a meeting with the managers of the Akron Pros, Cleveland Tigers, and Dayton Triangles. They wrote to every important football team in the Midwest and invited them to a meeting on September 17, 1920, at Hay's car dealership.

Representatives from ten teams showed up. There were so many men there that Hay could not fit them all in his office. They held the meeting in the automobile showroom, with some of the team reps sitting on the running boards of the cars.

As the men drank beer from a bucket, they decided not to have college players in the new league. The players would sign contracts with only one team, meaning that players could no longer jump from team to team. They also decided to call their new football league the American Professional Football Association (APFA) and make Jim Thorpe the league president.

One more thing: each team had to pay a hundred dollars to join the new league. But no one paid the money. Years later George Halas, who was at the meeting as the representative from the Decatur Staleys, said, "I doubt that there was a hundred bucks in the room."

They changed the name of the APFA a couple of years later to the National Football League. Why? "The other name stunk," Halas said.

So pro football and the NFL were underway. But the early years were not easy. No one played a regular schedule or the same number of games. The league did not keep statistics. News of the games rarely appeared in newspapers. There was no championship game at the end of the season. The league champion team was selected by a vote of the teams.

The NFL was way behind college football and professional baseball in popularity. The league needed something or someone to get people interested.

In the 1920s, baseball had Babe Ruth. The promise of the Babe's titanic home runs filled stadiums. Boxing had heavyweight champion Jack Dempsey. The "Manassa Mauler" fought before tens of thousands of fight fans for million-dollar purses. Golf had Bobby Jones. Even horse racing had its standout Thoroughbreds, such as Man o' War.

The NFL needed a star. Someone to get people talking about the new league and to get fans to come out to the parks and stadiums.

Luckily for the NFL, a star was about to arrive.

THE GALLOPING GHOST

*H*arold Edward "Red" Grange was born in Pennsylvania in 1903. But after his mother died when he was five years old, his father moved the family to Wheaton, Illinois.

Growing up without a mother was not easy. In the morning, Red milked the family cows, carried the milk to a creamery, then walked two miles to school.

With such a tough childhood, it's not surprising that Red fell in love with a tough game. He played football whenever he could. Pickup games around Wheaton. No helmets, no pads, and almost no rules.

Red became a terrific running back. He was five foot eleven and 175 pounds of fast-moving muscle. He was so shifty that other teams could barely touch him. At Wheaton High School, Red scored an unbelievable seventy-five touchdowns.

But when he arrived at the University of Illinois, he almost didn't try out for the football team. There were more than three hundred players hoping to make the squad, so Red walked away. He went back only because his friends forced him.

It was good that he did. Red's speed and sixth sense for would-be tacklers made him a threat to go all the way anytime he touched the ball. During his sophomore year in 1923, Red led Illinois to an undefeated season and the national championship. He scored twelve touchdowns and gained more than 1200 yards in just seven games.

The game against Michigan in his junior year made Red front-page news all over America. The undefeated Wolverines were one of the best teams in the country. Their defense had given up only two touchdowns in the last two seasons.

Illinois and Michigan fans packed the University of Illinois stadium to see what Red could do against a powerhouse. They didn't have to wait long. Michigan kicked off. Red took the ball at the five yard line, started to his left, cut to the right, and streaked past the shocked Wolverines to the end zone.

Touchdown!

Red touched the ball three more times in the first quarter. He scored each time! Once he zigzagged down the field on a sixty-seven-yard kickoff return, and two times he had breakaway runs of fifty-six and forty-four yards.

By the end of the game, Red had scored five touchdowns and gained more than four hundred yards. The Fighting Illini had shocked mighty Michigan, 39–14.

Red Grange was suddenly the stuff of legends. Sportswriters wrote poems about him, describing him as "a streak of fire" and "a breath of flame."

So when Red was ready to leave the University of Illinois in 1925, football fans wondered whether the "Galloping Ghost," as he was called, would turn pro.

Red signed with the Chicago Bears two days after his final college game.

Football fans came out in droves to see him. This was long before sports were on television. More than 39,000 fans packed Cubs Park—four times the usual crowd—to see the Bears play the Chicago Cardinals in Red's first pro game.

Then Red and the Bears went on a barnstorming tour of the East Coast, drawing even bigger crowds. Red and the Bears played eight games in eight different cities in just twelve days. More than 70,000 fans jammed the Polo Grounds in New York to see the Bears play the New York Giants. People came to see Red Grange but ended up falling in love with this new game—professional football.

Red and the game were suddenly in newspapers, magazines, and even the movies—Red starred in a 1926 movie called *One Minute to Play*.

Red hurt his knee in 1927. He still played but was never the "streak of fire" and "breath of flame" he had been in his days at Illinois.

But Red Grange had put professional football and the NFL on the map.

THE FIRST CHAMPIONSHIP GAME

George Halas had a problem. After the 1932 NFL season, the owner of the Chicago Bears wasn't sure his team would wind up as league champions.

The top of the final NFL standings looked like this:

1932 NFL STANDINGS

TEAM	WINS	LOSSES	TIES	PERCENTAGE
CHICAGO BEARS	6	1	6	.857
PORTSMOUTH SPARTANS	6	1	4	.857
GREEN BAY PACKERS	10	3	1	.769

The Chicago Bears and the Portsmouth Spartans had the same win and loss record—six wins and one loss. The Bears had six tie games and the Spartans had four. But under league rules, tie games did not count toward a team's record.

The NFL championship was usually awarded to the team with the best regular season record. Sometimes, however, the teams voted on which team was the champion.

Following the 1932 season, Halas convinced the league to have a championship playoff game between his Bears and the Spartans. The game would determine the league champion and make more money for the teams.

Halas insisted on holding this first championship game in Chicago on December 18 at Wrigley Field. He assured the league that he would have workers available to clear the field if it snowed.

Well, it snowed. In fact, there was a blizzard with zero-degree temperatures. The weather in Chicago was so terrible that the league moved the game indoors to Chicago Stadium, where the Chicago Black Hawks played hockey.

Chicago Stadium was not a regular football stadium. The field was only eighty yards long and forty-five yards wide (regulation NFL fields are 120 yards long and fifty-three yards wide). Worst of all, a circus had been in the stadium during the previous week. The field was covered with six inches of dirt . . . as well as a lot of stinky stuff left over from the circus horses and elephants.

Because the field was so small, the NFL made some rule changes for the game. For example, the teams kicked off from the ten yard line. Touchbacks came out to the ten yard line, not the twenty.

Another change was that if the ball went out of bounds, the next play started ten yards from the sideline. The rule at the time was if the ball went out of bounds, the next play started at the sideline and all the offensive linemen lined up on one side of the ball. The defense, of course, knew where the play was heading.

The 1932 championship game was a defensive struggle. The key play came on a fourth down with the Bears on the Spartans two yard line. Quarterback Carl Brumbaugh handed the ball to the Bears' star fullback, Bronko Nagurski. But Nagurski did not blast into the line. Instead the big man tossed a pass into the end zone to . . . Red Grange!

Touchdown! The Bears added a late safety and won 9–0.

Despite the bad weather and smelly field conditions, the game was a big hit. More than eleven thousand fans showed up for the contest. Better yet, the first NFL championship game was covered in newspapers and on radios around the country.

The NFL made some important rule changes following the 1932 championship. For example, they kept the idea of moving the ball in ten yards from the sidelines after a play where the ball had gone out of bounds.

The league also changed the passing rule so a player could throw the ball from anywhere in back of the line of scrimmage. Finally, the NFL placed the goalposts at the goal line instead of in back of the end zone. All these rules gave the offense a better chance of scoring touchdowns and field goals.

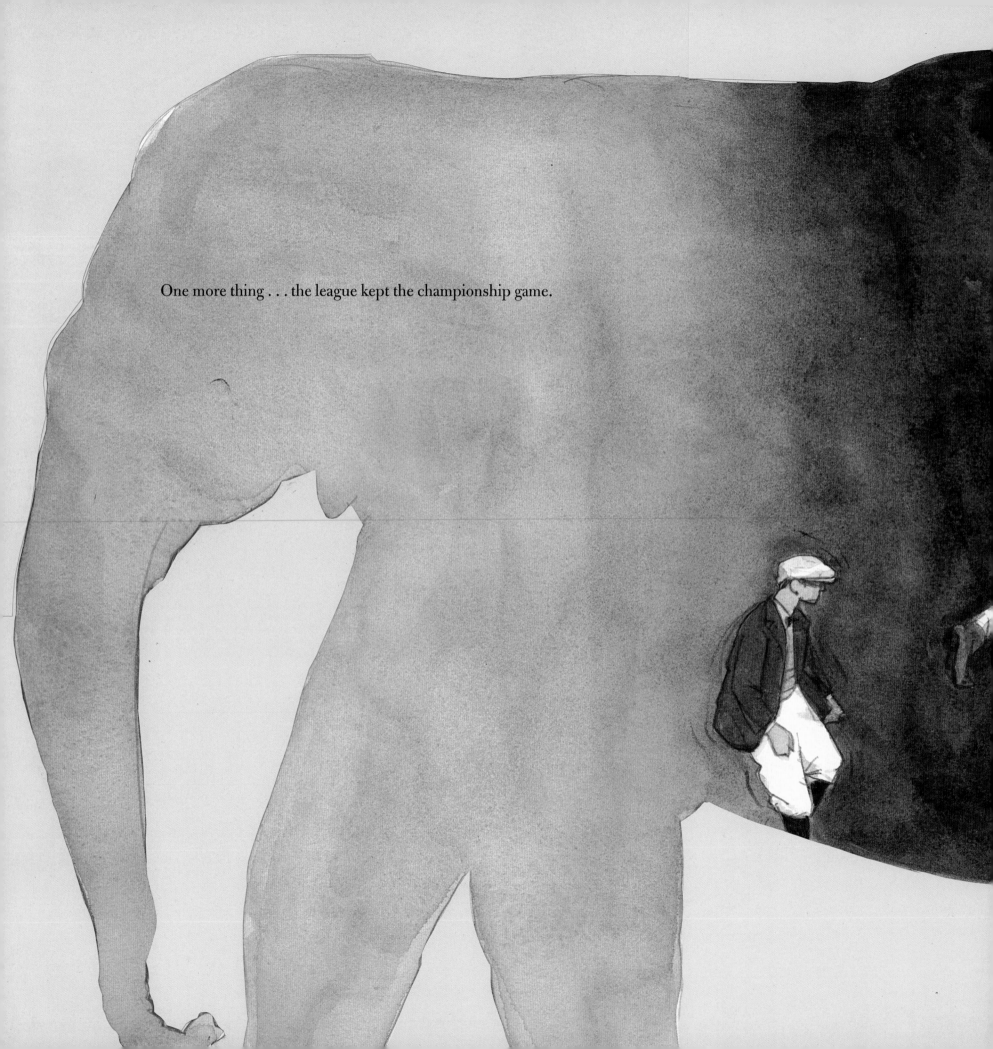

One more thing . . . the league kept the championship game.

FOOTBALL TAKES OFF

*T*he Carlisle Indian Industrial School set football free. That's right, a small school in southern Pennsylvania for the education of Native Americans changed the NFL.

In the early days, football was stuck on the ground. Teams ran plays into the line, turning the game into an ugly rugby scrum. Even after the forward pass was legalized in 1905, teams didn't use it often because there was a fifteen-yard penalty for any incompletion.

Carlisle and its coach, Glenn Scobey "Pop" Warner, changed that. The Carlisle Indians would fake runs and fling passes far downfield. In 1907 the Indians and their passing attack beat such traditional college powerhouses as Penn, Harvard, and the University of Chicago.

Slowly, other college teams started to pick up on Carlisle's style and pass more often (they also did away with the fifteen-yard penalty for incomplete passes). One of the first passers was Benny Friedman, who starred for the University of Michigan in the 1920s.

Friedman was only about five feet ten inches tall and about 180 pounds—but he was strong with huge hands. Growing up, Friedman did special exercises with a desk to make his right hand bigger. "I'd stretch my hand . . . till I could get it all the way across [the desk] and . . . have this big spread between my first finger and my thumb."

Friedman wrapped his big hands around the ball and threw perfect spirals. His passes were called "feather balls" because they were so easy to catch.

Friedman was a sensation when he went to the NFL. The triple-threat Friedman led the NFL in touchdown passes, running touchdowns, and extra points in 1928 for the Detroit Wolverines. Tim Mara, the owner of the New York Giants, bought the Detroit team just so he could get the Wolverines' star quarterback.

Benny didn't let his new team down. He threw twenty touchdown passes in his first season with the Giants. The Giants improved from a record of 4–7–2 in 1928 to 13–1–1 in 1929 with Friedman at the controls.

Other teams began to catch on. The NFL also changed the ball so it was slimmer and easier to throw. Quarterbacks such as Arnie Herber of the Green Bay Packers, Sid Luckman of the Chicago Bears, and "Slingin' Sammy" Baugh started filling Sunday afternoons with flying footballs. In 1947 Baugh threw 354 passes in just twelve games for almost three thousand yards.

The quarterbacks needed players who could catch all these passes. Don Hutson of the Green Bay Packers was one of the NFL's first great wide receivers. Hutson was lightning quick and tough as rawhide. They called him "the Alabama Antelope" because he was so fast and played his college ball at the University of Alabama.

Hutson was smart, too. He was the first receiver to run designed patterns—Z outs, buttonhooks, hook and goes. He also ran timing routes that were planned to the split second so the quarterback would know precisely where Hutson was going to be.

With his speed and precise patterns, no defensive back could cover him. Teams put two defensive backs on Hutson. But they still couldn't stop him.

In eleven seasons, Hutson led the NFL in receptions eight times and receiving yardage seven times. One season, Hutson caught seventy-four passes while the next highest receiver in the NFL caught twenty-seven. His record of ninety-nine career touchdowns stood for forty-four years following his retirement in 1945.

Don Hutson, Benny Friedman, Slingin' Sammy Baugh, and others changed the NFL. Now the game was not just played on the ground. Sundays saw the ball spinning through the air for gains of forty, fifty, and even more yards. The NFL was a place where anything could happen. A place where superstar quarterbacks such as Tom Brady, Peyton Manning, and Aaron Rodgers could throw for more than four hundred yards in a game.

And it all started with the Carlisle Indian Industrial School.

THE NFL AT WAR

*T*he 27,102 fans in Griffith Stadium in Washington, D.C., on December 7, 1941, hardly noticed the early announcement over the public address system.

"Admiral W. H. P. Blandy is asked to report to his office at once."

The fans were busy cheering their Redskins against the Philadelphia Eagles in the final game of the season. A few minutes later there was another announcement.

"The Resident Commissioner of the Philippines, Mr. Joaquín Elizalde, is urged to report to his office immediately."

Similar announcements were made for members of the FBI, United States Army, and even the president's Cabinet as the game continued. One wife sent a telegram to her husband, an editor at a large Washington newspaper, which was delivered to his seat in Section P, Box 37 on the thirty-five yard line. It read simply: *War with Japan. Get to office.*

Later, as the fans spilled out onto Georgia and Florida Avenues and into a changed world, they were not talking about the Redskins' 20–14 victory over the Eagles. The news had spread by word of mouth.

"Did you hear . . . ?"

"Japan attacked us . . . this morning. Killed about a couple thousand of our guys."

"Pearl Harbor . . . it's in Hawaii."

"I'm going downtown to enlist . . . right now."

The next day President Franklin D. Roosevelt went before a joint session of Congress and said, "Yesterday, December 7, 1941—a date which will live in infamy—the United States of America was suddenly and deliberately attacked by naval and air forces of the Empire of Japan."

The United States declared war on Japan and soon was fighting Adolph Hitler's Germany. World War II touched almost every corner of the globe. Over the next four years, more than 400,000 Americans were killed in the war. It is estimated that somewhere between 60 and 85 million people, soldiers and civilians, died worldwide because of the fighting.

The NFL went to war too. During the war, 638 NFL players served in the various branches of the military, 355 as officers.

Twenty NFL players were killed in action, including four All-Pros. One player, Jack Lummus, received the Medal of Honor, the highest military decoration given by the United States, for his heroism in the Battle of Iwo Jima in 1945.

First Lieutenant Lummus single-handedly charged and destroyed two Japanese fortified positions that were preventing his platoon from moving forward. He died from wounds he received during his heroic actions after telling a doctor, "The New York Giants lost a mighty good end today."

The NFL kept playing games, but with fewer players available, teams had to make major adjustments.

In 1943 the Pittsburgh Steelers merged with their archrivals, the Philadelphia Eagles. Fans dubbed the team the "Steagles." Even the joined rosters could not put the Steagles on top in the Eastern Division. They finished behind the Washington Redskins and the New York Giants.

The next season the Steelers merged with the Chicago Cardinals—sportswriters called them the Car-Pitts or carpets—with even less success. The Pittsburgh-Chicago team lost all ten of their games.

Teams were so desperate for players during the war, Chicago Bears coach George Halas recalled, that the Bears held an open tryout and signed "anyone who could run around the field twice."

Halas himself entered the navy in 1942 (he was forty-seven years old) and served as a lieutenant commander under Admiral Nimitz.

When the war ended in 1945, hundreds of former NFL players returned to the United States, eager to play again. Hundreds of college players who had entered the service instead of playing in the NFL also started thinking they would like to give the NFL a try.

In the years following World War II, the NFL was flooded with talent. The NFL was ready to get bigger and better.

SECOND
QUARTER

A FORGOTTEN DYNASTY

*L*ou "the Toe" Groza scraped the frozen turf with his shoe, trying to find a smooth spot on the sixteen yard line. The Cleveland Browns trailed the Los Angeles Rams 28–27 with twenty-eight seconds to play. A harsh wind swirled around Municipal Stadium, chilling the Christmas Eve crowd.

Groza looked up at the goalposts swaying in the wind and tried to imagine a tree in the middle. Just like the tree in Mindoro. Stationed in the Philippines during World War II, Groza had practiced his placekicking by kicking a football to the very top of a tree—because there were no goalposts in Mindoro.

He nodded to Otto Graham, the Browns quarterback and holder. The ball spun back. Groza stepped forward. The ball sailed, straight and true, between the uprights.

It was good! The Browns had won the 1950 championship game, 30–28. Head coach Paul Brown and the Cleveland Browns were the undisputed champions of pro football.

Growing up in Ohio, Paul Brown ate, slept, and drank football. As the quarterback for Massillon Washington High School, Brown was a coach on the field, calling plays and suggesting substitutions.

After playing at Miami University in Ohio, Brown decided not to go to law school. Instead he wanted to coach football.

He returned to Massillon, where he led the Tigers to an 80-8-2 record over nine seasons. He left to become the head coach at Ohio State. In his second season there, the thirty-four-year-old Brown led the Buckeyes to the national championship.

Still, Brown jumped at the chance to become the head coach of the Cleveland team in the new All-American

Football Conference (AAFC), a rival league to the NFL during the late 1940s. It was a chance to build a team from the ground up.

Brown built a winner. He accepted nothing less than success. Brown vetoed a vote to name the team the Panthers, after a failed minor league football team in Cleveland. "We don't want any association with a loser." Over his objection, the team became the Browns.

Brown hired six assistant coaches, instead of the usual two or three. He organized practices to the minute. The coaches studied film and worked year round. Brown organized his formations and plays into a playbook. Any player who did not know Brown's playbook backward and forward was gone.

Brown made sure he got the best players. He was the first coach with a system for scouting college players. Brown built his teams on speed. He timed players in the forty-yard dash, instead of a hundred yards, reasoning that players rarely ran more than forty yards during a game.

Remembering a tailback who led Northwestern to a rare win over Ohio State, Brown made Otto Graham his quarterback. Graham had not only played football at Northwestern, he also played basketball, as well as piano, violin, cornet, and French horn! Graham became the Browns' unquestioned leader on the field.

Brown even invented a single-bar face mask to protect his players, such as Graham, from facial injuries. Before that, NFL players wore helmets without face masks!

At a time when few African American players were in the NFL, Brown signed several key African American players. Marion Motley was a six-foot-one, 232-pound fullback who ran so hard he rattled the teeth of would-be tacklers. Bill Willis was small for a defensive lineman, at 213 pounds. But Willis was so quick, he was in the opponents' backfield before they knew it.

The Browns stormed through the AAFC, winning four consecutive championships. But when the Cleveland Browns (and the San Francisco 49ers and Baltimore Colts) moved from the AAFC to the NFL, fans thought the Browns wouldn't stand up to the stronger NFL teams.

They were wrong. Not only did the Browns win the NFL title in 1950, they returned to five more consecutive championship games, winning two more titles.

Others copied the Browns' success. Teams made their own playbooks. They studied film. More teams welcomed African American players.

Some of Paul Brown's assistant coaches and former players, such as Don Shula, Chuck Noll, and Bill Walsh, became championship head coaches. One assistant, Weeb Ewbank, took over the Baltimore Colts in 1954. Slowly, with the help of a former semipro quarterback, Ewbank molded the Colts into winners.

Just like Paul Brown and the Browns.

APFA CHAMPIONS (1920–1921)

1920 AKRON PROS	1921 CHICAGO STALEYS

NFL CHAMPIONS (1922–1932)

1922 CANTON BULLDOGS	1928 PROVIDENCE STEAM ROLLER
1923 CANTON BULLDOGS	1929 GREEN BAY PACKERS
1924 CLEVELAND BULLDOGS	1930 GREEN BAY PACKERS
1925 CHICAGO CARDINALS	1931 GREEN BAY PACKERS
1926 FRANKFORD YELLOW JACKETS	1932 CHICAGO BEARS
1927 NEW YORK GIANTS	

NFL CHAMPIONSHIP GAME WINNERS (1933–1966)

1933 CHICAGO BEARS	1950 CLEVELAND BROWNS
1934 NEW YORK GIANTS	1951 LOS ANGELES RAMS
1935 DETROIT LIONS	1952 DETROIT LIONS
1936 GREEN BAY PACKERS	1953 DETROIT LIONS
1937 WASHINGTON REDSKINS	1954 CLEVELAND BROWNS
1938 NEW YORK GIANTS	1955 CLEVELAND BROWNS
1939 GREEN BAY PACKERS	1956 NEW YORK GIANTS
1940 CHICAGO BEARS	1957 DETROIT LIONS
1941 CHICAGO BEARS	1958 BALTIMORE COLTS
1942 WASHINGTON REDSKINS	1959 BALTIMORE COLTS
1943 CHICAGO BEARS	1960 PHILADELPHIA EAGLES
1944 GREEN BAY PACKERS	1961 GREEN BAY PACKERS
1945 CLEVELAND RAMS	1962 GREEN BAY PACKERS
1946 CHICAGO BEARS	1963 CHICAGO BEARS
1947 CHICAGO CARDINALS	1964 CLEVELAND BROWNS
1948 PHILADELPHIA EAGLES	1965 GREEN BAY PACKERS
1949 PHILADELPHIA EAGLES	1966 GREEN BAY PACKERS

SUDDEN-DEATH OVERTIME

*J*ohnny Unitas and the Baltimore Colts had a long way to go.

Standing on their own fourteen yard line with only 2:20 remaining in the 1958 NFL championship game and trailing the New York Giants 17–14, the Colts realized their title hopes were fading fast.

That didn't bother Unitas. He had come a long way. A long way from shoveling coal as a kid for his family in Pittsburgh. A long way from being a 141-pound quarterback at St. Justin's High School.

Unitas played quarterback at the University of Louisville. But the Cardinals won just four games during his last two seasons. Unitas was only drafted in the ninth round by the Pittsburgh Steelers.

The Steelers cut him without much of a tryout. Unitas ended up playing semipro ball for the Bloomfield Rams for six dollars a game.

So Unitas wasn't worried when it was third-and-ten with everyone in Yankee Stadium screaming. He calmly tossed a pass to Lenny Moore, the Colts star halfback.

First down! The Colts were moving.

After an incompletion, Unitas went to his favorite receiver: Raymond Berry. Unitas had worked with Berry every day after practice when Unitas was a rookie and Berry was a second-year receiver, so Unitas could deliver the ball into Berry's sure hands the moment Berry cut into the open.

Soon the Yankee Stadium announcer was saying:

"Unitas to Berry for twenty-five yards and a first down."

"Unitas to Berry for fifteen yards and a first down."

"Unitas to Berry for twenty-two yards and a first down."

Sam Huff, the Giants All-Pro middle linebacker, said later, "Unitas to Berry . . . Unitas to Berry . . . Unitas to Berry. His voice echoed in my head."

The Colts had just enough time for a field goal. The team's field goal unit rushed out to line up a twenty-yard kick.

The ball spun back. The Baltimore kicker, Steve Myhra, took one step forward and the ball flew between the goalposts. Good!

The score was tied 17–17. For the first time in the history of the NFL, the championship game was going into overtime. Sudden-death overtime.

It was three days after Christmas and night was falling. The crowd of 64,185 was chilled to the bone, but no one was leaving.

More important, 45 million people had tuned in to watch the game. On black-and-white television sets all over America, they watched a game full of fumbles, goal-line stands, and last-second heroics, a heart-pounding drama played out in real time.

The Giants got the ball first but were forced to kick. Unitas trotted out with the ball on the twenty yard line. Eighty yards to go.

Mixing runs and passes, Unitas smartly moved the Colts to midfield. The Giants defense stiffened. They sacked Unitas for an eight-yard loss. It was third-and-fourteen and the Yankee Stadium crowd was on its feet.

Unitas faded back and looked for Moore on the right, but the Colts flanker was covered. Scrambling away from the swarming Giants defense, Unitas spied Berry, who had slipped past the secondary.

"Unitas to Berry for twenty-one yards and a first down."

The Giants defense was expecting a pass. Unitas fooled them and handed off to Alan Ameche. The Colts fullback rumbled twenty-three yards to the Giants nineteen yard line.

Now the Giants were expecting a run. Unitas fooled them again. Two passes put the ball on the one yard line.

Unitas stepped to the line of scrimmage. The desperate Giants defense dug in one more time.

"Blue twenty-five. Blue twenty-five. Hut, hut."

Unitas handed the ball to Ameche, who plunged through a hole in the Giants' line and landed in the end zone surrounded by a sea of flashing cameras.

Touchdown! The Colts won 23–17.

The Baltimore Colts were NFL champions, and 45 million people were now devoted NFL fans after watching one of the greatest games ever played.

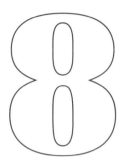

WINNING . . . THE ONLY THING

*T*he New York Giants walked out of Yankee Stadium with their heads hung low after their 23–17 overtime loss to the Baltimore Colts. One Giant was more disappointed than anyone: Assistant Coach Vince Lombardi.

Lombardi hated to lose. "Winning isn't everything," he once said. "It's the only thing."

Even back when he played football at Fordham University in the 1930s, Lombardi hated to lose. Although he was small (five feet eight inches, 180 pounds), Lombardi became a starter on Fordham's offensive line, known as the "Seven Blocks of Granite." He hated to lose when he coached at St. Cecilia High School in New Jersey and at West Point.

Of course, any team with Lombardi as a coach did a lot of winning. He designed the Giants offense that crushed the Chicago Bears 47–7 in the 1956 NFL championship game.

What Lombardi did not know as he left the field after the 1958 defeat was that he had coached his last game for the Giants. He was about to become the head coach and general manager of the Green Bay Packers—the losingest team in the NFL.

Green Bay had been a powerhouse in the 1930s and '40s. But the Packers had suffered through eleven consecutive losing seasons when Lombardi arrived in 1959. The Packers' record during the 1958 season was a dismal 1–10–1.

"I have never been associated with a loser and I don't expect to be now," Lombardi declared after accepting the Green Bay job.

Lombardi set out to change everything about the Packers. The players and everyone in the Green Bay front office would now be on "Lombardi time." That meant if you were not fifteen minutes *early* for practice or a meeting, you were late.

The players would be in top physical condition. Lombardi ran grueling practices so his players would not be tired at the end of the game. "Fatigue," he said, "makes cowards of us all."

Lombardi believed in hard work above all else. "The only place success comes before work is in the dictionary," he said.

Lombardi was also a genius at finding ways to motivate his men. Jerry Kramer, an All-Pro guard, revealed in his book *Instant Replay* that just when he was tired of Lombardi's criticism, the coach would put his arm around Kramer and tell him how important Kramer was to the team. Encouragement like that made Kramer and all the Packers want to play harder for "the Old Man."

Lombardi also simplified the Packers' playbook. He believed a team should practice certain plays again and again. The Packers ran their famed "Lombardi Power Sweep" with running backs Jim Taylor and Paul Hornung so often it became unstoppable.

Lombardi's coaching philosophy worked. In his first season, the Packers' record was 7–5, their first winning season since 1947. Lombardi was selected the NFL Coach of the Year.

Lombardi was not satisfied. He worked his team even harder. "The harder you work," he said, "the harder it is to surrender." In 1960, his second season, the Packers won the Western Conference and played in the NFL championship game.

They lost to the Philadelphia Eagles, 17–13. Lombardi looked at his players following the game and said, "This will never happen again. You will never lose another championship."

He was right. The Packers went on the greatest championship-winning streak in the history of the NFL. Led by a host of Hall of Fame players, the Packers dominated the New York Giants in the 1961 championship game, beating them 37–0. Green Bay won four more NFL championships (1962, 1965, 1966, and 1967) as well as the first two Super Bowls. Green Bay became "Titletown, USA."

Lombardi became a legend. America saw him as a coach who seemed to will greatness out of his teams and who embodied the traditional values of faith, loyalty, and hard work.

He's the coach whose name is on the Super Bowl trophy.

The Vince Lombardi Trophy.

CLEARING THE WAY

When Jim Brown stood on the stage to receive the first Associated Press Most Valuable Player (MVP) Award in 1957, he was not alone. Brown, who led the NFL in running yards and touchdowns as a rookie, was the first African American to win any NFL MVP award. But he was following many courageous black men who played in the early days of the NFL.

Men such as Frederick Douglass "Fritz" Pollard, an All-American tailback at Brown University in 1916. Pollard was small—five feet eight inches and only 155 pounds—but Walter Camp, the famous Yale coach, called him "the most elusive back of the year or of any year."

Pollard and Bobby Marshall were the first black players in the first season of the old American Professional Football Association. Pollard played for the Akron Pros and then played with and coached the Milwaukee Badgers, the Hammond Pros, and the Providence Steam Roller.

The next season there were a few more black players, including Paul Robeson, an All-American end from Rutgers. But Robeson didn't stay with pro football long. He went to Columbia Law School and became a world-famous actor and singer.

Any player has to be tough to play in the NFL. But the black players had to be extra tough. Back then, there was lots of discrimination against black people. In the South, blacks were not allowed in the same schools or hotels as whites and couldn't sit in the same section of the bus or use the same bathrooms. Things were better in the North, but not much better.

White players called black players every name in the book. But the worst part was that some white players tried to hurt black players on purpose. They stepped on their hands with their cleats or elbowed them in the mouth after the play was over.

From 1934 to 1946, there were no black players in the NFL. There wasn't any rule against them playing. But there was an understanding among the NFL owners not to allow them to play.

Some owners claimed black players weren't good enough for the NFL. But that wasn't true. Nine black college players were All-Americans between 1933 and 1946. Still, not one of those players was drafted, although the NFL drafted as many as two hundred players each year.

Kenny Washington, a record-breaking back at UCLA, was a player who didn't get drafted. In 1939 Washington led the nation in total yards and was a terrific defensive back, but still no NFL team drafted him in 1940.

For the next few seasons, Washington played in the Pacific Coast Football League, a minor league that allowed black players. Washington was the star of the league. He earned All-League honors every year he was in the PCFL.

Washington finally got his chance to play in the NFL in 1946. The Cleveland Rams had relocated to Los Angeles. The Rams agreed to sign African Americans after local black newspapers, as well as the city officials, pressured the team to integrate.

Washington was twenty-eight years old in 1946 and had undergone five knee surgeries when he became the first black player to sign a contract with an NFL team since the 1930s. He was not as fast as he had been at UCLA. Still, Washington was among the leading rushers in the NFL during the second of his three seasons.

Things changed slowly after that. Some black players signed and showed they belonged in the NFL. Marion Motley was a bruising All-Pro fullback for the Cleveland Browns. Bill Willis played on the Browns and was a cat-quick guard. Emlen Tunnell set records for interceptions with the New York Giants.

These early players cleared the way for Jim Brown . . . Gale Sayers . . . Jerry Rice . . . Lawrence Taylor . . . Reggie White . . . Walter Payton . . . Cam Newton . . . Julio Jones . . . Derrick Henry . . . and hundreds of other NFL players who showed that greatness does not depend on the color of a player's skin.

Charles Follis

Duke Slater

Bill Willis

Jim Brown

Marion Motley

Kenny Washington

Gale Sayers

Paul "Tank" Younger

Emlen Tunnell

Frederick Douglass "Fritz" Pollard

Barry Sanders

O. J. Simpson

Woody Strode

Walter Payton

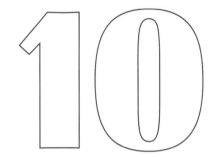

THE FIRST SUPER BOWL

They didn't call the first game the Super Bowl. It was the AFL-NFL World Championship Game.

But Lamar Hunt, the owner of the Kansas City Chiefs, knew the event needed a catchier name. When his kids told him about a high-bouncing ball called a Super Ball, that got Hunt thinking.

Super Ball . . . Super Bowl.

The name stuck. The Super Bowl in 1969 was officially called Super Bowl III.

Of course, lots of things were different in that first AFL-NFL World Championship Game on January 15, 1967.

The game wasn't a sellout. Everyone thought the NFL Green Bay Packers would crush the AFL Kansas City Chiefs. So there were more than thirty thousand empty seats in the Los Angeles Coliseum.

Tickets went for six dollars, ten dollars, and twelve dollars for the best seats in the house. Now Super Bowl tickets average about three thousand dollars—that is, if you are lucky enough to get them. The game always sells out.

There were questions about how to blend the two leagues. CBS had the contract to show NFL games, while NBC had the contract to show AFL games. Which television network would show the first game between NFL and AFL teams?

Both CBS and NBC showed the game. The two networks shared cameramen and equipment but aired the game on different channels.

Another problem: Which ball would the teams use? NFL teams played with a thicker Wilson ball called the Duke. Players thought it was better for kicking. AFL teams played with a thinner Spalding J5-V. Players thought it was better for passing.

The leagues compromised. When the Packers were on offense, they used the Duke. When the Chiefs were on offense, they used the AFL ball.

The first Super Bowl produced lots of excitement and the most unlikely hero in the history of the championship game.

Max McGee was a thirty-four-year-old wide receiver for the Packers who had caught only four passes for ninety-one yards during the 1966 regular season. McGee was so sure he wouldn't play in the first Super Bowl that he snuck out of his team's hotel on the night before the game and spent the late hours partying and having fun.

But on the third play of the game, the Packers star receiver, Boyd Dowler, hurt his shoulder.

"McGee," Packers coach Vince Lombardi shouted. "Go in for Dowler."

McGee looked around for his helmet. He had left it in the Packers' locker room!

"Here, Max," said Bob Long, another reserve wide receiver, handing McGee a helmet. "Use my helmet. . . . We'll send someone into the locker room to get yours."

With no sleep and the wrong helmet, McGee hustled onto the field and played the game of his life.

A few minutes after McGee entered the game, he slipped past Kansas City cornerback Willie Mitchell. Quarterback Bart Starr underthrew the ball, but McGee reached back and snagged it one-handed. He raced in for a thirty-seven-yard touchdown.

The Packers were up 7–0. But Kansas City battled back and trailed only 14–10 at halftime.

Green Bay put the game away when Max McGee struck again late in the third quarter. McGee beat Mitchell over the middle, and this time Starr put the ball right on McGee's numbers. The ball popped into the air, but McGee coolly gathered it in for another touchdown.

The Packers won 35–10.

Despite seven catches and two touchdowns, McGee was not the most valuable player of the game. That honor and a new Chevrolet Corvette went to the Packers quarterback, Bart Starr.

Maybe that was just as well. Starr raffled off the car by selling more than forty thousand one-dollar tickets. He used the money to help start a camp—Rawhide Boys Ranch—for at-risk kids.

The camp is still going strong outside Green Bay. Starr says the Corvette is still owned by someone in the city.

And the Super Bowl is the biggest sporting event in America.

THIRD
QUARTER

THE ICE BOWL

*L*ocated in northeast Wisconsin, the city and people of Green Bay are used to cold winters. Still, December 31, 1967, the day the Green Bay Packers played the Dallas Cowboys for the NFL title, was colder than usual.

The temperature read minus sixteen in the morning. As the sun rose it warmed up . . . to minus thirteen. The wind made it feel colder. The estimated wind chill was an unbelievable minus forty-six degrees.

All over the city, cars could not start, their engines frozen solid. The turf at Lambeau Field was frozen too, as hard and unforgiving as a marble tabletop.

Willie Wood, the Packers All-Pro safety, thought they would never play the game in such frigid weather. But they played. The Packers and Cowboys played one of the most unforgettable games in NFL history.

The Green Bay fans came ready for the cold. Here is a list of the clothing one fan, Bob Kaminski, wore to the game.

On his feet: socks, work shoes, woolen socks over the shoes, then galoshes over everything.

On his lower body: long johns, flannel pajamas, work overalls.

On his upper body: a T-shirt, flannel shirt, insulated sweat shirt, heavy parka.

On his head: face mask with holes for mouth and eyes, wool hat.

Then Kaminski climbed into a sleeping bag and sat with foam rubber at his feet and on his seat.

He saw a back-and-forth thriller. The Packers jumped out to an early lead on two touchdown passes from quarterback Bart Starr to wide receiver Boyd Dowler.

The Cowboys did not give up. Defensive end Willie Townes sacked Starr, causing a fumble. George Andrie, Dallas's other defensive end, scooped up the ball and rumbled in for a touchdown. The Cowboys had cut the lead in half, 14–7. Dallas added a field goal, and so the Packers led 14–10 at halftime.

The second half was as cold as the first. A game official had his whistle freeze to his lips when he left it in his mouth. Packer linebacker Ray Nitschke was getting frostbite on his feet. Up in the press box, the writers' portable typewriters sat frozen to the ledge.

Down on the field, the Cowboys grabbed a 17–14 lead on a trick play. Halfback Dan Reeves tossed a wobbly pass to flanker Lance Rentzel, who slipped behind the Green Bay secondary for the score.

The sun was sinking lower, and so were the chances of the Packers winning their third straight NFL championship. Green Bay got the ball one last time on the thirty-two yard line. Sixty-eight yards to go with 4:50 remaining.

Bart Starr walked calmly into the Green Bay huddle. "This is it," the quarterback told his team. "We're going in."

Mixing passes and runs, the Packers moved the ball into Dallas territory with two minutes to go. Fullback Chuck Mercein told Starr, "I'm open on the left if you need me." Starr tossed a pass that Mercein reached back and grabbed with his icy fingers. He raced to the eleven yard line.

Two more runs drove the ball to the Cowboys one yard line. First down with less than a minute to play.

Another run. No gain. Time-out.

On the next play, running back Donny Anderson slipped on the frozen field. No gain again. Green Bay called time-out.

Third down. The ball on the one yard line. Sixteen seconds to go, but the Packers did not have any time-outs. Time for one more play.

Packer coach Vince Lombardi did not even discuss a field goal to tie the game. "Run to win," was Lombardi's motto.

Lombardi and Starr decided on 31 Wedge, a quarterback sneak. Packer guard Jerry Kramer blasted forward, pushing back Jethro Pugh, the Dallas tackle, just far enough for Starr to slip into the end zone.

Touchdown! Green Bay had won the "Ice Bowl" 21–17.

I GUARANTEE IT

"**H**ey, I got news for you. We're going to win the game. I guarantee it."

The hundreds of fans who crowded into the Touchdown Club in Miami on Thursday, January 9, 1969, thought Joe Namath was crazy. The twenty-five-year-old New York Jets quarterback with the long hair and fancy white football shoes had guaranteed that his American Football League (AFL) team would beat the NFL champion Baltimore Colts and win Super Bowl III.

Didn't Namath know . . .

- The Colts were 15–1 and had shut out the Cleveland Browns 34–0 for the NFL championship.
- According to Jimmy "the Greek" Snyder, the Colts had the "greatest defensive team in the history of football."
- The Las Vegas oddsmakers had made the Colts an eighteen-point favorite.
- Almost every sportswriter in the country was predicting a Colts victory.

Namath, however, had been studying game films and knew in his heart that his younger, faster Jets could beat the older, slower Colts. Namath also suspected the day had arrived when the AFL teams were as good as the NFL teams. Maybe better.

In the late 1950s the NFL had twelve teams. Rich men, such as oilmen Lamar Hunt and Bud Adams,

wanted to buy teams in the league. But the NFL owners would not sell, and the league had no plans to expand. So Hunt contacted all the men and cities that wanted NFL teams and started his own league. "We called ourselves the Foolish Club," he recalled. They later called themselves the American Football League. The AFL was born in 1960 with eight teams.

At first AFL teams did not play against NFL teams, but they competed with the older league to draft and sign college players. This competition drove the salaries teams paid players sky high. In 1965 Joe Namath signed a contract worth the then unheard-of price of $427,000. (Now the minimum NFL salary is more.)

Soon veteran NFL players started to follow the money to the AFL. In 1966, after years of more expensive contracts, the NFL and AFL decided to merge the two leagues into one big league by 1970.

The two leagues remained separate from 1966 to 1970, playing each other only in the Super Bowl and later in preseason games.

Like an older brother, the NFL thought it was the better league. After all, the Green Bay Packers had won the first two Super Bowls easily, beating the Kansas City Chiefs 35–10 and the Oakland Raiders 33–14. The NFL also won most of the preseason matchups.

Everyone knew the NFL was better than the AFL. Everyone, that is, except Namath and the Jets. The Jets head coach, Weeb Ewbank, confidently told his team before Super Bowl III, "When we win, don't carry me off the field. I have a bad hip and I don't want to get hurt."

Mixing short passes and runs by Matt Snell, Namath proved the Jets could move the ball against the tough Colts defense. When the Colts tried to blitz, Namath's lightning-quick release allowed him to get rid of the ball before getting tackled.

Early in the second quarter, Namath led the Jets on an eighty-yard march that ended with Snell dashing past the Colts line on a four-yard run. The Jets were ahead 7–0.

The Jets added to their lead with field goals by Jim Turner.

10–0 . . . 13–0 . . . 16–0 . . .

Anytime the Colts seemed ready to get back in the game, they would fumble, miss a field goal, or throw an interception. Namath coolly ate up yardage and the clock when the Jets had the ball.

Slowly, the sellout crowd of 75,377 who had packed the Orange Bowl in Miami began to realize some startling new truths.

The Jets were the better team.

The AFL was as good as the NFL.

And Joe Namath wasn't crazy when he guaranteed a New York victory.

13

THE IMMACULATE RECEPTION

*A*rt Rooney was ready to give up.

The seventy-one-year-old owner of the Pittsburgh Steelers, who everyone called "the Chief," had made his money betting on racehorses. Rooney had used $2500 of that racetrack money in 1933 to buy an NFL franchise for his beloved hometown of Pittsburgh. It had seemed like a good bet.

But the team became lovable losers. Since 1933, Rooney and the Pittsburgh fans had enjoyed only a handful of winning seasons and no championships.

So Rooney, the old horseplayer, knew something about the odds and long shots. He knew there were days when someone else held the winning ticket.

December 23, 1972, looked like one of those days. The Steelers trailed 7–6 in a playoff game against the Oakland Raiders. The winner would go to the AFC championship and have a chance to play in the Super Bowl.

But time was running out. Pittsburgh had the ball on its own forty yard line with only one minute and thirteen seconds to go. The Steelers young quarterback, Terry Bradshaw, threw three desperate incompletions. The ball was still on the forty yard line, but now there were only twenty-two seconds left.

The Chief calculated the odds. No chance. So Rooney stood and said goodbye to his friends in his owner's box. Head down, he got into a nearby elevator for a silent ride to the Steelers' locker room.

"I figured we had lost," Rooney said later, "and I wanted to get to the locker room early so I could personally thank all the players for the fine job they'd done all season."

Back on the field, Coach Chuck Noll wasn't ready to give up. He called one more play—66 Circle Option.

Bradshaw would try to throw the ball to wide receiver Barry Pearson.

Bradshaw scrambled to his right. He couldn't find Pearson. But he spied Steelers running back John "Frenchy" Fuqua breaking into the clear near the Oakland thirty-five yard line. It was worth a gamble. . . .

Bradshaw zipped a pass toward Fuqua just as a Raiders defensive lineman slammed the Steelers quarterback to the ground.

Franco Harris, the Steelers star rookie running back, was supposed to block for Bradshaw. But when Bradshaw scrambled, Harris drifted out, hoping Bradshaw would throw to him. When Bradshaw threw to Fuqua, Harris kept running downfield.

Jack Tatum, the Oakland Raiders free safety, had his eye on Fuqua too. Tatum smashed into Fuqua just as Bradshaw's pass arrived. *Crack!*

The ball flew out, tumbling toward the turf. Oakland defensive back Jimmy Warren raised his hands in celebration. But only for a moment.

Harris, who was still running down the field, saw the ball coming end over end toward him. *This is it!* he thought. Harris grabbed the ball with the edges of his fingertips just before it touched the ground. He never broke stride, stiff-arming Warren and sprinting into the end zone.

Touchdown!

When Art Rooney emerged from the silence of the elevator, he turned left toward the Pittsburgh locker room. A stadium guard stopped him.

"You won it!" the guard shouted.

"Are you kidding?" the puzzled Chief asked.

"Listen to the crowd."

As the sound of the jubilant Pittsburgh football fans echoed through the stadium, the Chief realized his greatest long shot had come in. A hundred-to-one shot. A never-in-a-million-years shot.

The Steelers didn't win the Super Bowl that year. But the team went on to win four championships in the next seven years. And the NFL would see more amazing comebacks, such as when the New England Patriots scored twenty-five unanswered points in the second half and six points in overtime to win Super Bowl LI. There were Hail Mary passes. Fingertip catches with time running out. Drives down the field in the last desperate seconds that brought fans to their feet.

But none of those comebacks would be more amazing than the play Pittsburgh fans saw a few days before Christmas in 1972.

The play football fans still call "The Immaculate Reception."

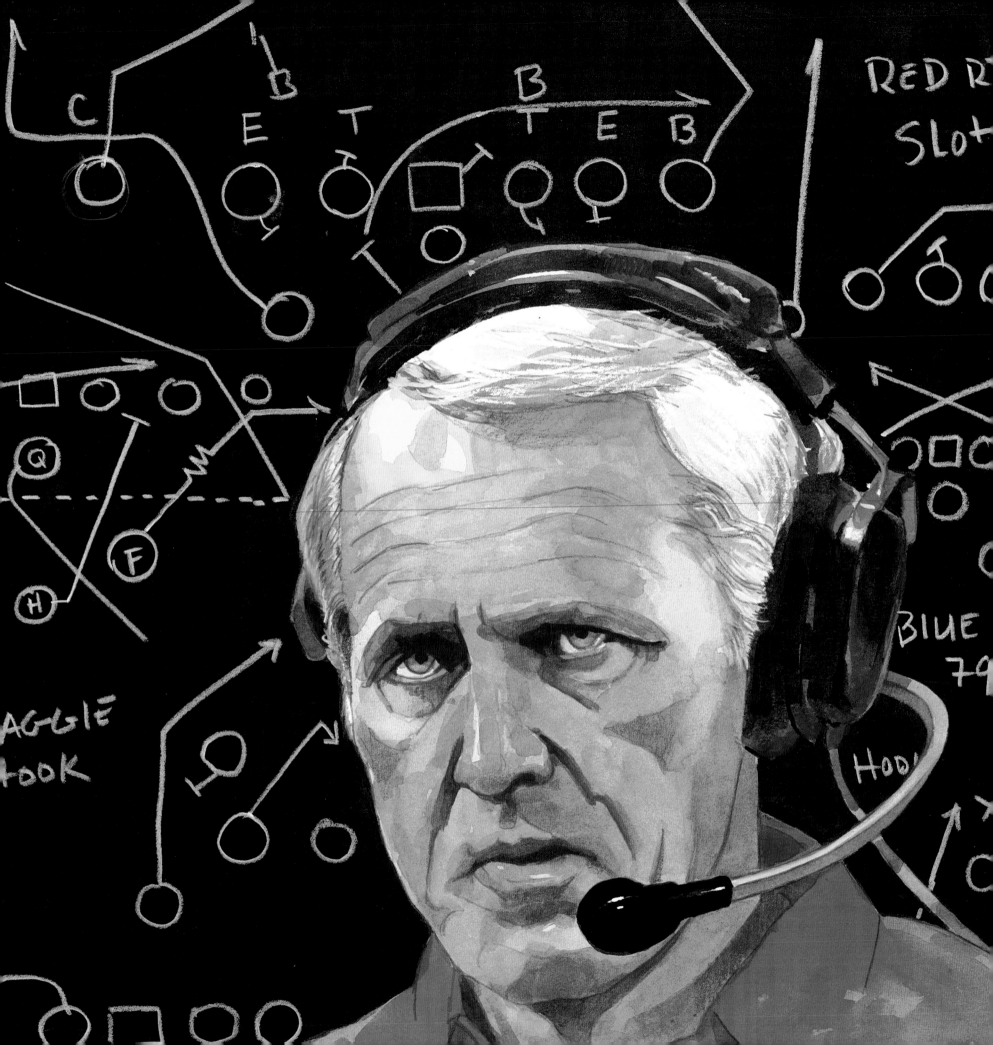

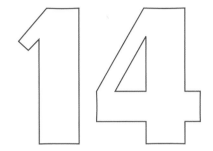

WEST COAST OFFENSE

*B*ill Walsh wasn't sure what he could do.

    The quarterback coach of the Cincinnati Bengals did not have a quarterback. Not a real NFL quarterback. The kind of quarterback who was tall and strong and had a rifle for a right arm.

A Joe Namath. Or even a rookie like Terry Bradshaw.

No, Walsh had Virgil Carter. The kid out of Brigham Young University with the popgun arm was no Joe Namath.

Still, the Bengals head coach, the legendary Paul Brown of the Cleveland Browns, wanted Walsh to come up with something to get the Bengals passing attack going.

Walsh came up with something: a brand-new kind of offense.

Until the 1970s, NFL teams, such as the champion Green Bay Packers, established the run to set up the pass. Teams passed mostly on third down or when they were behind, long downfield passes to one or two wide receivers. It was fine if a quarterback completed 50 percent of his passes.

Walsh changed that. He made the pass, not the run, the Bengals' main offensive weapon. The Bengals passed on any down to keep their opponent guessing.

But not long passes. Carter's passes wobbled past twenty yards. Walsh had Carter throw short passes. Five-, ten-, or fifteen-yard passes. Quick, perfectly timed tosses before the defense could sack the quarterback.

Slants. Posts. Quick hitches. Flares to the sidelines. Patterns that made the defense cover the whole field.

Another thing . . . Walsh sent out four or even five receivers almost every play. He used tight ends and running backs swinging out of the backfield. If you wanted to play for Bill Walsh, you had better be able to catch the ball.

And it worked. Walsh coached three quarterbacks while he was with the Bengals—Carter, Greg Cook, and Ken Anderson. None of them were Hall of Famers, but each one was among the leading quarterbacks in the NFL at least one season.

Because it wasn't the quarterbacks . . . it was the offense.

Walsh took his offense to Stanford for two seasons. Then to the San Francisco 49ers.

The 49ers were 2–14 in 1979, Walsh's first year. But they were getting better, especially on offense. Most important, Walsh drafted a quarterback with skinny legs from Notre Dame: Joe Montana.

Montana did not have a strong arm, but he was accurate. Montana dropped back on dancer's feet and put the ball on the money every time.

One more thing . . . nothing bothered Montana. Joe Cool. That's what they called him. Joe Cool.

In Walsh's third year at San Francisco, Montana took the 49ers and their quick-strike offense all the way to Super Bowl XVI, where they beat the Cincinnati Bengals 26–21. But Walsh didn't stop there. He kept drafting better players. Players who fit his offense.

Walsh took Roger Craig, a do-everything halfback from Nebraska, in the second round of the NFL draft. Craig became the first player in the NFL to gain more than a thousand yards rushing and a thousand yards receiving in one season.

Two years later Walsh drafted Jerry Rice, a wide receiver from the tiny Division I-AA school of Mississippi Valley State. Rice had run up big numbers in college playing against small-time teams such as Southern University and Kentucky State. Some experts thought Rice would never make it in the NFL.

But Rice was perfect for Walsh's offense. He was quick, ran precise patterns, and seemed completely in tune with Montana. Rice also had strong hands that he had developed growing up laying bricks with his father in northeast Mississippi.

Walsh's 49ers went on to win Super Bowls XIX and XXIII. Walsh retired, but the 49ers kept going, winning Super Bowls XXIV and XXIX.

Walsh's offense kept going too. Super Bowl champions such as the Green Bay Packers, the Denver Broncos, and the Tampa Bay Buccaneers all used Walsh's ideas.

Short, quick passes all over the field. The West Coast offense. An offense that kept the scoreboard clicking by passing the ball.

The offense that changed the NFL.

ALL-TIME NFL RECEIVING LEADERS
THROUGH 2018–2019 SEASON

RANK	PLAYER	YARDS	YEARS
1	JERRY RICE*	22,895	1985–2004
2	LARRY FITZGERALD	16,279	2004–2018
3	TERRELL OWENS*	15,934	1996–2010
4	RANDY MOSS*	15,292	1998–2012
5	ISAAC BRUCE	15,208	1994–2009
6	TONY GONZALEZ*	15,127	1997–2013
7	TIM BROWN*	14,934	1988–2004
8	STEVE SMITH	14,731	2001–2016
9	MARVIN HARRISON*	14,580	1996–2008
10	REGGIE WAYNE	14,345	2001–2014
11	ANDRE JOHNSON	14,185	2003–2016
12	JAMES LOFTON*	14,004	1978–1993
13	CRIS CARTER*	13,899	1987–2002
14	ANQUAN BOLDIN	13,779	2003–2016
15	HENRY ELLARD	13,777	1983–1998
16	TORRY HOLT	13,382	1999–2009
17	ANDRE REED*	13,198	1985–2000
18	STEVE LARGENT*	13,089	1976–1989
19	IRVING FRYAR	12,785	1984–2000
20	ART MONK*	12,721	1980–1995
21	JASON WITTEN	12,448	2003–2017
22	BRANDON MARSHALL	12,351	2006–2018
23	JIMMY SMITH	12,287	1992–2005
24	CHARLIE JOINER*	12,146	1969–1986
25	HINES WARD	12,083	1998–2011

*INDUCTED INTO THE PRO FOOTBALL HALL OF FAME

THE GROUND GAME

*I*t's the simplest play in football. The quarterback turns and hands the ball to the running back. Or maybe he pitches it to him.

Simple: get the ball to the running back and let him run. It's a play that has been in every football game from the day Rutgers beat Princeton 6–4 in 1869 to NFL games today.

The hard part is finding a running back.

The running back has to be fast to get away from tacklers. Strong to run through them. Rugged to take all the hits. There have been many kinds of running backs in the NFL.

THE BATTERING RAMS

He was born Bronislau Nagurski in Rainy River, Canada, a piece of cold country north of Minnesota. As a running back (and linebacker) for the Chicago Bears in the 1930s, they called him Bronko. The name fit Nagurski's straight-up-the-gut running.

They called Earl Campbell "the Tyler Rose" because his hometown of Tyler, Texas, was famous for its roses. But there was nothing pretty about the Houston Oilers running back. With thighs the size of a man's waist, Campbell never went around tacklers; he went through them.

THE SCATBACK

Gale Sayers—"the Kansas Comet"—scored a record twenty-two touchdowns during his rookie season with the Chicago Bears. With his breakaway speed and ankle-twisting moves, defenders could barely lay

a hand on Sayers, whether he was running out of the backfield or running back kicks.

One opponent said, "Trying to bring Sayers down is like going rabbit hunting without a gun."

Barry Sanders never gained less than 1100 yards in a season, and usually much more, during his ten-year career with the Detroit Lions. Whenever Sanders scored a touchdown—and he scored 109—he just handed the ball to the official. No wild celebrations. Sanders knew he would be coming back.

THE GLIDERS

Sometimes after the defense tackled Dallas Cowboy running back Emmitt Smith, the players would trade high fives only to find out Smith had gained another seven yards. Smith gained yardage so easily, it seemed he hadn't gone that far. Smith always got his yards—18,355 in all, more than any running back in NFL history.

In 1984 Eric Dickerson ran for 2,105 yards, the most in a single NFL season, by barely stirring the air. "He made no noise when he ran," his coach John Robinson of the Los Angeles Rams said. "He's the smoothest runner I've ever seen."

THE VERY BEST

Sometimes a running back has it all. The size, the speed, the moves, the toughness.

Jim Brown was big—six foot two and 232 pounds—at a time when defensive linemen were barely bigger. But Brown was fast. He had been a track star at Syracuse University.

That combination made Brown almost unstoppable. He led the NFL in rushing yards eight of the nine seasons he played, averaging more than five yards a carry for his career. But perhaps Brown's most amazing statistic was that despite the countless hard hits he endured, he never missed a single game.

Walter Payton was not as big as Jim Brown—five foot ten and two hundred pounds. But he made himself rock solid by running up a steeply angled fifty-yard black dirt hill in Arlington Heights, near Chicago. Payton called that dirt hill a "goal setter" and a "will maker." That hill was the secret of Payton's ability to keep going for 16,726 rushing yards and another 4,538 yards on 492 catches.

There were many more great runners through the years . . . Ernie Nevers, Marion Motley, Jim Taylor, Tony "TD" Dorsett, Marcus Allen, Marshall Faulk, Adrian Peterson. Up to the great running backs of today . . . Ezekiel Elliott, Todd Gurley, and Mark Ingram.

Just give them the ball and let them run. Simple.

ALL-TIME NFL RUSHING LEADERS
THROUGH 2018–2019 SEASON

RANK	PLAYER	YARDS	YEARS
1	EMMITT SMITH*	18,355	1990–2004
2	WALTER PAYTON*	16,726	1975–1987
3	BARRY SANDERS*	15,269	1989–1998
4	FRANK GORE	14,748	2005–2018
5	CURTIS MARTIN*	14,101	1995–2005
6	LADAINIAN TOMLINSON*	13,684	2001–2011
7	JEROME BETTIS*	13,662	1993–2005
8	ADRIAN PETERSON	13,318	2007–2018
9	ERIC DICKERSON	13,259	1983–1993
10	TONY DORSETT*	12,739	1977–1988
11	JIM BROWN*	12,312	1957–1965
12	MARSHALL FAULK*	12,279	1994–2005
13	EDGERRIN JAMES	12,246	1999–2009
14	MARCUS ALLEN*	12,243	1982–1997
15	FRANCO HARRIS*	12,120	1972–1984
16	THURMAN THOMAS*	12,074	1988–2000
17	FRED TAYLOR	11,695	1998–2010
18	STEVEN JACKSON	11,438	2004–2015
19	JOHN RIGGINS*	11,352	1971–1985
20	COREY DILLON	11,241	1997–2006
21	O. J. SIMPSON*	11,236	1969–1979
22	WARRICK DUNN	10,967	1997–2008
23	RICKY WATTERS	10,643	1992–2001
24	JAMAL LEWIS	10,607	2000–2009
25	LESEAN MCCOY	10,606	2009–2018

*INDUCTED INTO THE PRO FOOTBALL HALL OF FAME

FOURTH
QUARTER

16

CONCRETE CHARLIE

*T*he Green Bay Packers trailed the Philadelphia Eagles 17–13 in the 1960 NFL championship game. The ball was on the Eagles twenty-two yard line. There was time for the Packers to run one, maybe two more plays.

Bart Starr faded back and tossed the ball to Jim Taylor coming out of the backfield. The big fullback rumbled inside the ten yard line, where he was met head-on by Chuck Bednarik. The thirty-five-year-old linebacker, known as "Concrete Charlie," stopped Taylor cold and tossed him to the Franklin Field turf.

Taylor tried to scramble to his feet, hoping the Packers could run one more play. But Bednarik held Taylor down with his massive arms as the last seconds ticked away. Finally Concrete Charlie got up and walked off the field . . . a champion.

And the last man to play an entire NFL game.

That's right. Bednarik had been on the gridiron for all but three plays on that chilly December afternoon. "I didn't run down on kickoffs, that's all," he recalled years later. Bednarik played offensive center and linebacker—right in the middle of the action.

In the early days of the NFL, team rosters were small and players played both offense and defense. In 1925 only sixteen players suited up for an NFL game.

Gradually, the teams grew larger. By 1938, teams dressed thirty players for each game. Still, players often played offense and defense. Some were terrific at both.

One season, quarterback Sammy Baugh of the Washington Redskins led the NFL by completing

55.6 percent of his passes. Baugh was also the team's punter. He led the NFL by averaging 45.9 yards a kick. Slingin' Sammy wasn't done. He led the NFL in interceptions, too, picking off eleven passes.

During World War II (1941–45), there were fewer football players because hundreds were fighting overseas. The ones who were around weren't in good shape. So the league allowed more substitutions.

In 1949 the league adopted a rule that allowed unlimited substitutions. Now different groups of players could play on offense, defense, or special teams. The age of two-platoon football and the specialist was born.

Still, change came slowly. Coaches wanted players who had more than one skill. In that 1960 championship between the Packers and the Eagles, the Packers halfback, Paul Hornung, was also the team's field-goal kicker. Max McGee, who caught a touchdown pass, was the Packers punter.

Lou "the Toe" Groza was a six-foot-three, 240-pound offensive and defensive lineman during his twenty-one-year career (1946–67) with the Cleveland Browns. But Groza was also the Browns field goal kicker. He split the uprights for 264 career field goals.

With expanding rosters—forty active players in 1964, forty-three in 1975, and now forty-six—coaches started to keep players who could do one thing very well.

Pete and Charlie Gogolak were not really American football players. The brothers were soccer players who were born in Hungary. But the Gogolak brothers could kick. Their success at putting the ball through the uprights ushered in scores of foreign, soccer-style kickers such as Garo Yepremian (Cyprus), Tony Zendejas (Mexico), and Jan Stenerud (Norway).

Punters became specialists too. Ray Guy played for the Oakland and Los Angeles Raiders from 1973 to 1986. He punted the ball more than a thousand times while doing hardly anything else. But he kicked his way into the Pro Football Hall of Fame.

Now the kicking game is so important that teams keep a "long snapper," such as Jon Weeks of the Houston Texans, whose only job is to snap the ball accurately to the punter and to the holder for field goals.

There are third-down backs, such as Alvin Kamara, who gain almost as many yards catching passes as running from scrimmage. The defense has its own specialists too—pass-rushing ends, such as Julius Peppers, as well as defensive backs called nickelbacks to defend against the pass.

With more specialists, the NFL game is faster, more precise, and more exciting.

And no place for Concrete Charlie.

GET THE QUARTERBACK

*O*ne second . . . two seconds . . . three seconds . . .

That's about the time an NFL quarterback has to fade back, locate his receivers, set his feet, and throw the ball. On time and on target.

That's a lot to do in three seconds. Especially when bodies are flying all around and seventy thousand people are screaming.

Three seconds.

If the quarterback has less time, he probably won't have time to set his feet. He may throw the ball too quickly. Chances are the pass will be incomplete or even intercepted.

More than three seconds? That will give the quarterback's receivers time to find some open space downfield. Chances are better the pass will be completed and maybe go for a touchdown.

Then the crowd goes wild, the receiver celebrates in the end zone, and the quarterback walks off the field . . . a hero.

The defensive line and linebackers try to hurry the quarterback. The offensive line tries to protect the quarterback and give him time to throw.

It has been that way since Benny Friedman and Arnie Herber were slinging passes for the New York Giants and Green Bay Packers in the 1930s. It is even truer today, when NFL quarterbacks such as Russell Wilson and Matthew Stafford throw forty and sometimes fifty times a game.

So NFL coaches and scouts are always looking for players who are strong enough and fast enough to get to the quarterback.

David "Deacon" Jones did not go to a big-time football college such as Notre Dame or Alabama. Jones played at a historically black college called Mississippi Vocational College (now Mississippi Valley State).

But when scouts from the Los Angeles Rams saw the six-foot-five, 272-pound Jones outracing running backs, they thought he might be worth a late pick.

Wow, were they right! Picked in the fourteenth round of the 1961 NFL draft, Jones went on to become a five-time All-Pro as a member of the famous Rams defensive line called "the Fearsome Foursome."

Jones specialized in terrorizing NFL quarterbacks. He tackled quarterbacks so often in the backfield that he is credited with inventing the football term "sack" (although others credit an NFL publicist for the term).

The NFL did not begin to keep statistics for sacks until 1982, eight years after Jones retired. However, it is estimated Jones had more than 170 career sacks, including three seasons when he had twenty sacks or more.

Lawrence "LT" Taylor revolutionized the position of linebacker when he played from 1981 to 1993 for the New York Giants. By blitzing and turning linebackers into pass rushers, Taylor made life miserable for NFL quarterbacks.

At six foot three and 240 pounds, and with a sprinter's speed, Taylor was fast enough to run past slower offensive linemen and strong enough to blast through running backs assigned to block him. LT was a nightmare for any coach trying to design an offense.

Bill Walsh, the Super Bowl–winning coach of the San Francisco 49ers, stayed up late trying to design schemes to stop Taylor. Eventually, Walsh concluded he had to find a new kind of offensive tackle. One big enough but also fleet-footed enough to handle Taylor.

Soon everyone in the NFL was searching for this new kind of tackle. Men like Walter Jones, Anthony Munoz, Jonathan Ogden, and Tyron Smith. Huge men who could still move quickly enough to keep pass rushers such as JJ Watt and DeMarcus Ware off their quarterback.

Pressure the quarterback. Protect the quarterback.

Find a pass rusher. Draft a pass blocker.

This back-and-forth of football has been going on ever since the Carlisle Indians figured out it was easier to move the football through the air than over the ground.

One second . . . two seconds . . . three seconds . . .

It isn't much time, but it can mean the whole game.

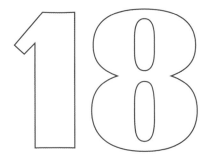

THE DRAFT: THEN AND NOW

*T*he seats in the AT&T Stadium are filled with football fans wearing their favorite teams' jerseys. Some are in costume or greasepaint. Millions more are watching on television. Weeks of talk and speculation are about to end.

Roger Goodell, the commissioner of the NFL, steps to the microphone.

"With the first pick of the 2018 NFL draft, the Cleveland Browns select Baker Mayfield, quarterback of Oklahoma."

The Browns fans in the AT&T Stadium burst into cheers. The television networks roll highlight films of Mayfield scrambling and throwing for touchdowns. NFL draft experts immediately begin to analyze whether the Browns have picked a winner or have made a big mistake.

It's the NFL draft, a three-day extravaganza that gets more attention than most NFL games.

The draft, where NFL franchises pick college players, was not always such a big deal. For the first fifteen years of the league, the NFL did not have a draft. Teams simply recruited players, and every team had a chance to sign any player. The problem was the best players tended to go to the best teams.

So Bert Bell, the owner of the Philadelphia Eagles, whose team was struggling to win games, had an idea in 1935. A player draft.

Teams would pick college players, and the player could only sign a contract with the team that picked him. The team with the worst record would pick first (Philadelphia had the worst record in 1935). The other teams would pick according to their record, with the best team picking last.

The NFL owners agreed. They held the first NFL draft at the Ritz-Carlton Hotel in Philadelphia on February 8, 1936.

The first draft was nothing like the draft now. There were . . .

No television cameras, no fans, no scouting reports, no players hanging around backstage, and no so-called draft experts.

The nine team owners posted on the hotel room wall a list of ninety college players who would be eligible to play professional football. Then they started picking.

The owners had only a vague idea of who the college players were. Some owners looked at magazines or consulted newspaper articles with lists of All-American or All-Conference teams.

The Eagles chose Jay Berwanger, a halfback from the University of Chicago. Berwanger had just received the first Heisman Trophy as the outstanding college football player in 1935.

Berwanger never played in the NFL. In fact, only thirty-one of the eighty-one players drafted (the first draft was nine rounds) signed with NFL teams. In 1936 college football was much more popular than the NFL, and the pros did not pay their players that much money. The poor Philadelphia Eagles—the team that came up with the idea for the draft—didn't sign a single player they drafted in 1936.

But as the years went by, the draft changed when teams started to recognize the importance of picking the best players. Following World War II, some teams hired scouts, who traveled the country to watch college games and talk with coaches. In the 1960s, the Dallas Cowboys used computers to help organize their information about college players.

By the 1980s, the NFL held its first official scouting combine. That's where college athletes are tested for speed, strength, and athletic ability. The teams even give them a written test to see how smart they are.

In 1980 ESPN, the new all-sports network, asked the NFL if it could televise its "selection meeting." The NFL commissioner, Pete Rozelle, thought it was a stupid idea. Who would want to watch a business meeting?

Boy, was Rozelle wrong. Now more than 45 million fans tune in to some part of the NFL draft to hear the commissioner say . . .

"With the second pick of the 2018 NFL draft, the New York Giants select Saquon Barkley, running back of Penn State."

IRON MIKE

*T*hey called him "Iron Mike."

Mike Webster was short for an NFL lineman. But he had thick arms and legs, perfect for moving huge defensive linemen.

Webster was smart, too. As the Steelers offensive center, he had to recognize the different defensive formations and bark out signals to his fellow linemen. The center is the leader, the quarterback, of the offensive line.

Everyone thought Iron Mike was indestructible. He played in more than 340 NFL games in his seventeen-year career, counting preseason and postseason games. Webster won four Super Bowl rings with the Pittsburgh Steelers. He missed only four games despite being in the middle of the mayhem along the line of scrimmage.

But after Webster retired from the NFL, things changed. He seemed lost without football. Over the years, he lost his jobs, his money, his home, and his family. Sometimes Webster would sleep in a truck or an old train station.

He took painkillers to ease the aches of his old football injuries. Pills for his back as well as his knees, ankles, fingers, and shoulders. Webster took pills for headaches, too. Unending headaches that followed him around like a dark cloud.

The man who knew the Steelers playbook backward and forward could not think straight. Webster kept notes on yellow pads and wrote letters to friends, but the notes and letters did not make sense.

His old Steelers teammates tried to help, but mostly they wondered: What had happened to Iron Mike?

Iron Mike had a secret. The secret was only revealed after he died.

"Who is Mike Webster?" Dr. Bennet Omalu asked in 2002 when the body of a fifty-year-old man was brought into the Allegheny County, Pennsylvania, medical examiner's office. Dr. Omalu's office mates laughed. Mike Webster was famous in Pittsburgh. He was an All-Pro center for the Steelers' four Super Bowl championship teams. Everyone knew Iron Mike.

Dr. Omalu, however, had been born in Nigeria, on the west coast of Africa. He followed soccer, not football.

Dr. Omalu's job was to find out why Webster had died. People said he was an athlete, but Webster was in terrible shape and looked much older than fifty.

Dr. Omalu examined Webster from the top of his head to the tips of his toes. Suspecting a possible head injury, he got permission to examine Webster's brain by cutting the tissue into thin slices and studying the tissue under a microscope.

That was when Dr. Omalu discovered Webster's secret. Iron Mike wasn't really Iron Mike at all. He wasn't indestructible.

Staring into the microscope, Dr. Omalu saw brown patches in sections of Webster's brain. He knew from examining thousands of brains that the brown patches were not normal. The brown patches were the reasons Mike Webster's brain had not been working properly. Dr. Omalu said the hundreds, even thousands of hits a football player takes over the years were the cause.

At first no one wanted to believe the Nigerian doctor. The NFL and its doctors said he was wrong.

Mike Webster was the first of many NFL players to be diagnosed with the brain injury CTE, chronic traumatic encephalopathy. Doctors, including Dr. Ann McKee at Boston University, examined the brains of more NFL players and found that they, too, had CTE. They continue to study CTE.

Over the years the list of NFL players who doctors discovered suffered from CTE grew. The list included some of the greatest players in the history of the NFL. Junior Seau. Kenny "the Snake" Stabler. Frank Gifford. Bubba Smith. John Mackey.

By 2017, the list of former NFL players determined to have suffered from CTE included more than 100 names. The NFL donated millions to the study of CTE. The league outlawed helmet-to-helmet hits and became much more careful with players who suffer concussions.

Still, there were questions surrounding the game.

Is it safe to play football?

Why do some players get CTE and others do not?

Can the game be changed to make it safer?

But there's one question no one asks anymore: What happened to Iron Mike?

ALMOST PERFECT

Nobody's perfect.

The old saying is true in the NFL. Except for one year . . . and one team. Then there was the year when a team was almost better than that.

The 1972 Miami Dolphins were not a glamorous team. The Dolphins beat their opponents with a grind-it-out offense that featured three top running backs.

Larry Csonka was a bruising fullback who gained the tough yards and kept the first-down chains moving. Eugene "Mercury" Morris was a breakaway threat on running plays, passes, and kick returns. Jim Kiick was not quite as good as his two teammates, but he could run, block, and catch passes.

The Dolphin quarterbacks, Bob Greise and Earl Morrall, did not throw often—Miami threw only eleven passes in their 14–7 Super Bowl win over the Washington Redskins that year. The Dolphins gained 884 more yards on the ground than in the air during the regular season.

Combine this dependable offense with a rock-solid defense, and Miami had the formula for a perfect season. The Dolphins ran the table in 1972: seventeen wins, no losses. Undefeated, untied, and unmatched.

But at Super Bowl XLII in Phoenix, it looked like the New England Patriots might pass the 1972 Miami Dolphins. The Patriots quarterback Tom Brady had tossed a touchdown pass to Randy Moss to pull New England ahead of the New York Giants 14–10, with only 2:39 left.

New England had stormed through the 2007 regular season and playoffs, posting an 18–0 record before the Super Bowl. The Patriots were nothing like the Dolphins. New England was an aerial circus, with a

high-scoring offense that averaged almost thirty-seven points a game during the season. Brady threw for 4,806 yards and an eye-popping fifty touchdowns.

Now if the Patriots could hang on, they would be 19–0, even better than the Dolphins.

Following the Patriots' kickoff, the Giants had the ball on their own forty-four yard line. Third down, five yards to go, with only 1:15 remaining. The Giants needed a first down . . . and more.

The Giants quarterback, Eli Manning, called the play—62 Y Sail Union. Four receivers spread out across the field.

Manning faded back. But the Patriots defense crashed in. Two Patriot linemen grabbed Manning, but the quarterback wriggled free, stumbling five steps back and to his right. He spotted David Tyree, who had caught just four passes for thirty-five yards during the regular season, down the middle of the field.

Manning squared his shoulders and let a forty-yard pass fly. "If it had been the third quarter . . . I would not have thrown the ball," Manning recalled later. "But it was third-and-five, I almost got sacked, so you either throw it away or you give Tyree a shot. I gave him a shot."

Tyree leaped for the ball with Patriots safety Rodney Harrison draped on him like an overcoat. The two players came down wrestling for the ball, Tyree's hand pinning the football against the white N and Y letters on his blue helmet.

Completed pass! First down Giants at the Patriots twenty-four yard line, with only fifty-nine seconds left.

A couple of plays later, Giants wide receiver Plaxico Burress split out to the left. He ran straight at the New England cornerback and then broke hard for the left corner of the end zone.

The cornerback slipped and tried to catch up. The ball was already in the air. Manning's pass settled into Burress's arms just inside the end zone.

Touchdown!

The Giants were ahead 17–14. Now it was New England's turn to hope for a miracle. But the Giants had used up all the day's miracles.

The Patriots were not perfect anymore. New England would win a record six Super Bowls in all, but Super Bowl XLII had slipped away. It had taken David Tyree's incredible catch—a play that Steve Sabol, former president of NFL Films, called "the greatest play in Super Bowl history"—to beat them.

Nobody's perfect . . . except the Dolphins. And almost the Patriots.

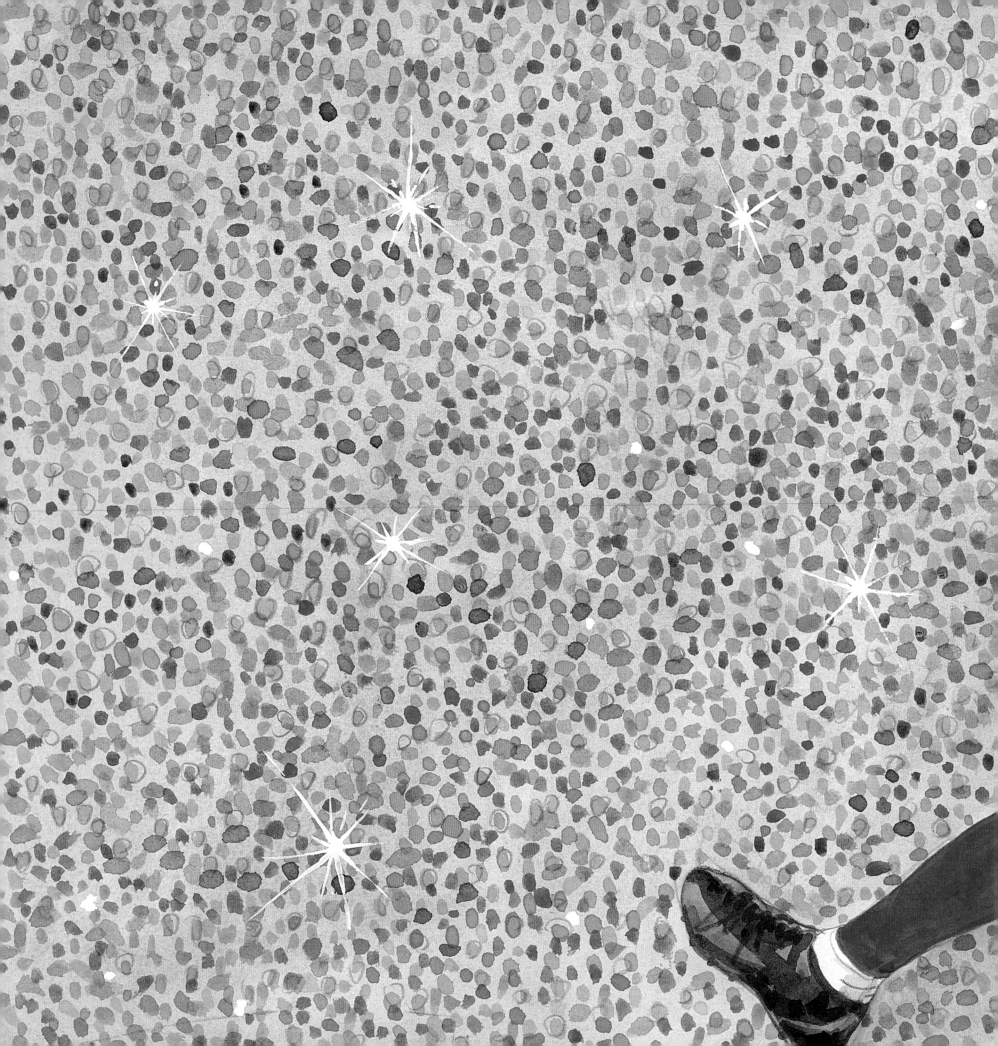

POSTGAME
SHOW

*A*ll the stories of the gridiron add up to one incredible story: how the NFL got to where it is today. Remember, it all started in Canton, Ohio. A bunch of guys who loved the new game called professional football got together and drank beer out of a bucket and tried to make the game better.

Now when the owners of NFL teams get together, it is in the gleaming NFL headquarters on Park Avenue in the middle of Manhattan or in some five-star hotel.

And the teams at that first meeting . . .

Akron Pros	Hammond Pros
Canton Bulldogs	Muncie Flyers
Cleveland Tigers	Racine Cardinals
Dayton Triangles	Rochester Jeffersons
Decatur Staleys	Rock Island Independents

. . . were mostly small midwestern towns playing on local high school fields. Now the NFL has teams in thirty-two of the biggest cities in the United States. The games are played in huge, multimillion-dollar stadiums that seat tens of thousands of fans. Some NFL games are even played in London and Mexico City.

And remember when it cost a hundred dollars—about the cost of an official NFL football today—to get into the league? Now NFL franchises are worth billions of dollars. The last NFL team to be sold, the Carolina Panthers, was sold for $2.2 billion.

Some experts estimate that the bigger, more popular franchises such as the Dallas Cowboys may be worth as much as four billion dollars. That is a lot of hundred-dollar bills. Forty million, to be exact.

A hundred years ago, almost no one paid any attention to the NFL and professional football. It was long before television, but the games were rarely written up in the newspapers. The NFL did not even keep official statistics until the 1932 season.

Now the NFL is everywhere. Nineteen of the twenty most watched television shows in history are Super Bowl broadcasts. Some of the most watched weekly shows on television are NFL games. Millions of fans play fantasy football and follow every touchdown scored and yard gained in the NFL.

Finally, look around at the millions of kids (and adults) wearing their favorite team shirts. A number 4 Dak Prescott Cowboys jersey. Or number 13 in the Cleveland Browns colors for Odell Beckham Jr. Or Carson Wentz's Eagles number 11.

Or the fans who are flying their team's flag from their house or car. Or carting their books to school in an official team backpack.

Yes, the NFL is everywhere.

And a long way from Ralph Hay's automobile showroom.

LIST OF SUPER BOWL CHAMPIONS (1967–2019)

NUMBER	CHAMPION	OPPONENT	SCORE
I	GREEN BAY PACKERS	KANSAS CITY CHIEFS	35-10
II	GREEN BAY PACKERS	OAKLAND RAIDERS	33-14
III	NEW YORK JETS	BALTIMORE COLTS	16-7
IV	KANSAS CITY CHIEFS	MINNESOTA VIKINGS	23-7
V	BALTIMORE COLTS	DALLAS COWBOYS	16-13
VI	DALLAS COWBOYS	MIAMI DOLPHINS	24-3
VII	MIAMI DOLPHINS	WASHINGTON REDSKINS	14-7
VIII	MIAMI DOLPHINS	MINNESOTA VIKINGS	24-7
IX	PITTSBURGH STEELERS	MINNESOTA VIKINGS	16-6
X	PITTSBURGH STEELERS	DALLAS COWBOYS	21-17
XI	OAKLAND RAIDERS	MINNESOTA VIKINGS	32-14
XII	DALLAS COWBOYS	DENVER BRONCOS	27-10
XIII	PITTSBURGH STEELERS	DALLAS COWBOYS	35-31
XIV	PITTSBURGH STEELERS	LOS ANGELES RAMS	31-19
XV	OAKLAND RAIDERS	PHILADELPHIA EAGLES	27-10
XVI	SAN FRANCISCO 49ERS	CINCINNATI BENGALS	26-21
XVII	WASHINGTON REDSKINS	MIAMI DOLPHINS	27-17
XVIII	LOS ANGELES RAIDERS	WASHINGTON REDSKINS	38-9
XIX	SAN FRANCISCO 49ERS	MIAMI DOLPHINS	38-16
XX	CHICAGO BEARS	NEW ENGLAND PATRIOTS	46-10
XXI	NEW YORK GIANTS	DENVER BRONCOS	39-20
XXII	WASHINGTON REDSKINS	DENVER BRONCOS	42-10
XXIII	SAN FRANCISCO 49ERS	CINCINNATI BENGALS	20-16
XXIV	SAN FRANCISCO 49ERS	DENVER BRONCOS	55-10
XXV	NEW YORK GIANTS	BUFFALO BILLS	20-19

NUMBER	CHAMPION	OPPONENT	SCORE
XXVI	WASHINGTON REDSKINS	BUFFALO BILLS	37-24
XXVII	DALLAS COWBOYS	BUFFALO BILLS	52-17
XXVIII	DALLAS COWBOYS	BUFFALO BILLS	30-13
XXIX	SAN FRANCISCO 49ERS	SAN DIEGO CHARGERS	49-26
XXX	DALLAS COWBOYS	PITTSBURGH STEELERS	27-17
XXXI	GREEN BAY PACKERS	NEW ENGLAND PATRIOTS	35-21
XXXII	DENVER BRONCOS	GREEN BAY PACKERS	31-24
XXXIII	DENVER BRONCOS	ATLANTA FALCONS	34-19
XXXIV	ST. LOUIS RAMS	TENNESSEE TITANS	23-16
XXXV	BALTIMORE RAVENS	NEW YORK GIANTS	34-7
XXXVI	NEW ENGLAND PATRIOTS	ST. LOUIS RAMS	20-17
XXXVII	TAMPA BAY BUCCANEERS	OAKLAND RAIDERS	48-21
XXXVIII	NEW ENGLAND PATRIOTS	CAROLINA PANTHERS	32-29
XXXIX	NEW ENGLAND PATRIOTS	PHILADELPHIA EAGLES	24-21
XL	PITTSBURGH STEELERS	SEATTLE SEAHAWKS	21-10
XLI	INDIANAPOLIS COLTS	CHICAGO BEARS	29-17
XLII	NEW YORK GIANTS	NEW ENGLAND PATRIOTS	17-14
XLIII	PITTSBURGH STEELERS	ARIZONA CARDINALS	27-23
XLIV	NEW ORLEANS SAINTS	INDIANAPOLIS COLTS	31-17
XLV	GREEN BAY PACKERS	PITTSBURGH STEELERS	31-25
XLVI	NEW YORK GIANTS	NEW ENGLAND PATRIOTS	21-17
XLVII	BALTIMORE RAVENS	SAN FRANCISCO 49ERS	34-31
XLVIII	SEATTLE SEAHAWKS	DENVER BRONCOS	43-8
XLIX	NEW ENGLAND PATRIOTS	SEATTLE SEAHAWKS	28-24
50	DENVER BRONCOS	CAROLINA PANTHERS	24-10
LI	NEW ENGLAND PATRIOTS	ATLANTA FALCONS	34-28 (OT)
LII	PHILADELPHIA EAGLES	NEW ENGLAND PATRIOTS	41-33
LIII	NEW ENGLAND PATRIOTS	LOS ANGELES RAMS	13-3

INDEX

BIBLIOGRAPHY

Numerous books and articles were used in writing this book, including those listed below.

BOOKS

Barber, Phil, and John Fawaz. *NFL's Greatest: Pro Football's Best Players, Teams, and Games.* London: Dorling Kindersley, 2000.

Bowden, Mark. *The Best Game Ever: Giants vs. Colts, 1958, and the Birth of the Modern NFL.* New York: Atlantic Monthly Press, 2008.

Callahan, Tom. *Johnny U: The Life and Times of John Unitas.* New York: Crown Publishers, 2006.

Daly, Dan. *The National Forgotten League: Entertaining Stories and Observations from Pro Football's First Fifty Years.* Lincoln: University of Nebraska Press, 2012.

Easterbrook, Gregg. *The King of Sports: Football's Impact on America.* New York: Thomas Dunne Books, 2013.

Editors of *Sports Illustrated. Football's Greatest.* Bill Syken, ed. New York: *Sports Illustrated*, 2012.

Editors of *Sports Illustrated Kids. Football: Then to Wow!* Des Moines, IA: *Sports Illustrated Kids*, 2014.

Freeman, Mike. *Jim Brown: The Fierce Life of an American Hero.* New York: William Morrow Publishers, 2006.

Frommer, Harvey. *When It Was Just a Game: Remembering the First Super Bowl.* Lanham, MD: Taylor Trade Publishing, 2015.

Garner, Joe, and Bob Costas. *100 Yards of Glory: The Greatest Moments in NFL History.* New York: Houghton Mifflin Harcourt, 2011.

Greenberg, Murray. *Passing Game: Benny Friedman and the Transformation of Football.* New York: PublicAffairs, 2008.

Harris, David. *The Genius: How Bill Walsh Reinvented Football and Created an NFL Dynasty.* New York: Random House, 2008.

Jenkins, Sally. *The Real All Americans: The Team That Changed a Game, a People, a Nation.* New York: Broadway Books, 2008.

Kramer, Jerry, and Dick Schaap. *Instant Replay: The Green Bay Diary of Jerry Kramer.* Reprint ed. New York: Doubleday, 2006.

Kriegel, Mark. *Namath: A Biography.* New York: Penguin Books, 2005.

Lahman, Sean. *The Pro Football Historical Abstract: A Hardcore Fan's Guide to All-Time Player Rankings.* Guilford, CT: Lyons Press, 2008.

Lewis, Michael. *The Blind Side: Evolution of a Game.* Reprint ed. New York: W. W. Norton, 2007.

MacCambridge, Michael. *America's Game: The Epic Story of How Pro Football Captured a Nation.* Reprint ed. New York: Anchor Books, 2005.

Madden, John, with Bill Gutman. *John Madden's Heroes of Football: The Story of America's Game.* New York: Dutton Books, 2006.

Maraniss, David. *When Pride Still Mattered: A Life of Vince Lombardi.* New York: Touchstone, 2000.

Peterson, Robert W. *Pigskin: The Early Years of Pro Football.* Reprint ed. New York: Oxford University Press, 1997.

Pomerantz, Gary M. *Their Life's Work: The Brotherhood of the 1970s Pittsburgh Steelers.* Reprint ed. New York: Simon & Schuster Paperbacks, 2014.

Poole, Gary Andrew. *The Galloping Ghost: Red Grange, an American Football Legend.* New York: Houghton Mifflin Harcourt, 2008.

Povich, Shirley. *All Those Mornings . . . At the Post.* New York: PublicAffairs, 2005.

Reyburn, Susan, and the Library of Congress. *Football Nation: Four Hundred Years of America's Game.* New York: Harry N. Abrams, 2013.

Stewart, Wayne. *Remembering the Stars of the NFL Glory Years: An Inside Look at the Golden Age of Football.* Lanham, MD: Rowman & Littlefield, 2017.

Weiss, Don, with Chuck Day. *The Making of the Super Bowl: The Inside Story of the World's Greatest Sporting Event.* New York: McGraw-Hill, 2002.

Williams, Pete. *The Draft: A Year Inside the NFL's Search for Talent.* New York: St. Martin's Press, 2006.

ARTICLES

Beschloss, Michael. "T.R.'s Son Inspired Him to Help Rescue Football." History Source, *New York Times,* August 1, 2014.

Bieler, Des. "Super Bowl LII Had Fewest Viewers Since 2009, Down 7 Percent from Last Year." *Washington Post,* February 5, 2018.

Goldstein, Richard. "Deacon Jones Dies at 74; Made Quarterback Sack Brutal and Enthralling." *New York Times,* June 4, 2013.

Layden, Tim. "Print the Legend." *Sports Illustrated,* February 8, 2016.

Morrison, Jim. "The Early History of Football's Forward Pass." Smithsonian.com, December 28, 2010.

In addition, many websites were consulted, especially *Pro Football Reference*: pro-football-reference.com.

ENDPAPERS

First row, from left to right:
SEAN PAYTON: The winningest coach in New Orleans Saints history, he led the Saints to victory in Super Bowl XLIV. • BART STARR: Hall of Fame quarterback for the Green Bay Packers, he led them to three consecutive NFL championships in 1965–1967 and won the first two Super Bowls. • DEACON JONES: Hall of Fame defensive end selected to eight Pro Bowls and twice named NFL Defensive Player of the Year. His #75 was retired by the Los Angeles Rams. • DOUG WILLIAMS: Led the Washington Redskins to victory as quarterback in Super Bowl XXII, for which he was named Super Bowl MVP. • BILL PARCELLS: Hall of Fame head coach who led the New York Giants to two Super Bowl victories (XXI, XXV) and later coached the Patriots, Jets, and Cowboys. • CURTIS MARTIN: Five-time Pro Bowl running back who starred for the New York Jets, who retired his #28. He led the league in rushing in 2004 and was inducted into the Hall of Fame.

Second row, from left to right:
PEYTON MANNING: One of the greatest quarterbacks of all time, fourteen-time Pro Bowl selection, five-time NFL MVP, two-time Super Bowl champion (XLI, 50), he had his #18 retired by both the Colts and Broncos. • DON SHULA: Winningest coach in Miami Dolphins history, he won Super Bowls VII and VIII, the latter during the only undefeated season in league history. Hall of Fame inductee. • DAN MARINO: Retired from the Dolphins in 1999 as the holder of numerous league records as quarterback. A nine-time Pro Bowl selection and the 1984 NFL MVP, he is a Hall of Fame inductee and had his #13 retired by the Dolphins. • O. J. SIMPSON: Although his criminal trials and conviction later overshadowed his playing career as a running back, he was named the 1973 NFL MVP, retired with the second-most rushing yards in league history, and was inducted into the Hall of Fame. • JOHN MADDEN: Hall of Fame head coach of the Oakland Raiders, winning Super Bowl XI, he later became an award–winning sportscaster, writer, and namesake of the popular *Madden NFL* gaming franchise. • LAWRENCE TAYLOR: A fearsome linebacker, ten-time Pro Bowl selection, two-time Super Bowl champion with the Giants (XXI, XXV), 1986 NFL MVP, three-time Defensive Player of the Year, and Hall of Fame inductee.

Third row, from left to right:
RAY LEWIS: Hall of Fame linebacker who played his entire career for the Baltimore Ravens, winning two Super Bowls (XXXV, XLVII), Super Bowl XXXV MVP, thirteen Pro Bowl selections, and two Defensive Player of the Year awards. • JERRY RICE: The greatest wide receiver in league history by many measures, he won three Super Bowls with the San Francisco 49ers (XXIII, XXIV, XXIX), was Super Bowl XXIII MVP, selected thirteen times to the Pro Bowl, named Offensive Player of the Year twice, had his #80 retired by the 49ers, and was inducted into the Hall of Fame. • PETE CARROLL: Innovative head coach who led the Seattle Seahawks to victory in Super Bowl XLVIII. • PHILIP RIVERS: Stalwart quarterback of the Los Angeles Chargers who holds many franchise records for passing and was selected to eight Pro Bowls. • DREW BREES: Long-time quarterback for the New Orleans Saints, champion and MVP of Super Bowl XLIV, twelve-time Pro Bowl selection, and holder of many league records for passing. • AARON RODGERS: An exceptionally accurate and prolific quarterback, led the Packers to victory in Super Bowl XLV and was named Super Bowl MVP in addition to twice being named NFL MVP.

DEDICATIONS

For the Marblehead Golf Crowd:
Alan, Benny, Jay, Kenny, Lee, Sal, Shubie, and Sully.
Great teammates, better friends. —F. B.

To my Miami Dolphins and their coach Brian Flores,
the late linebacker Nick Buoniconti, and all the seasons
of ups, downs, and excitement since 1972. —J. E. R.

ACKNOWLEDGMENTS

I am grateful to everyone at Simon & Schuster for supporting my idea to create a book that celebrates the world's greatest sport. *Gridiron* is my thanks to all the football players who have made the ultimate sacrifice and given me over forty years of pure pigskin pleasure.

Special thanks to writer Fred Bowen for his wonderful manuscript. And to my editor, Giants fan Karen Wojtyla, and to Caitlyn Dlouhy for connecting us. And to art director extraordinaire Sonia Chaghatzbanian and designer Michael McCartney. And a profound thanks to my amazing wife, Lesa Cline-Ransome, whom I love dearly despite the fact that she is a Patriots fan.

Shout-out to the Pro Football Hall of Fame in Canton, Ohio, which provided me with invaluable research and inspiration. And finally, to my indomitable Miami Dolphins, with whom I fell in love back in 1972.

—James E. Ransome